Reluctant Hero

Reluctant Hero

A Novel

By

Betty Freeman Haines

InterWorld Publishing Inc.

Though inspired by actual events, this novel is a work of fiction. Details of the events, locations and characters were filtered, altered, and created from my childhood memories, folklore, family tales, memories of my siblings, and by my imagination. Any resemblance to a real person, living or dead is entirely coincidental.

ISBN: **978-0-615-33436-3**

Table of Contents

For
My Children - Who adored him

Rick Platt
Brandi Kuhlmann
John (Freeman) Platt

"A man's worth is not reckoned by his diplomas or his money; rather it is his integrity that determines his true worth."

-Author's paraphrase of Richard Paul Evans in *The Letter*

Acknowledgments

Accolades to my dear husband and best friend; Vern, you never once complained about the hours I spent at my PC; you kindly covered many of the cooking and cleaning chores and even fetched me endless cups of tea. Without your understanding and support, I would surely have given up long before I finished writing this novel. Thank you, sweetheart, you really are something special.

I owe a huge debt of gratitude to my dear brother who inspired me to write this novel. Clay, the memories you shared are a treasure beyond words; your encouragement, support, proof reading, suggestions, and unfailing faith during the creation of this novel, were very special gifts and you gave them so very graciously. Thanks!

My sister generously shared her memories. Mary, I suspect that you thought I had taken leave of my senses when I told you that I was writing this novel. Thanks for not saying so and for trusting that I would do it right, if I did it at all. You have always been there for me and I love you for it.

Kudos to my former HP manager and mentor, Peter R. Kimball. Pete, you told me on a number of occasions that I possessed more talent and ability than I was utilizing. You were brave enough to walk your talk and assign projects and opportunities that encouraged me to learn for myself how right you were. I owe you more than a few words of gratitude in this book can ever repay; you helped me develop the self-confidence to reach for and embrace new experiences, and I am eternally grateful. By the way, Pete, your extensive vocabulary and love of words always inspired and intrigued me – you are without a doubt the greatest wordsmith I ever met. I hope I have made you proud.

Many thanks go to my sister-in-law Barbara, my brother-in-law Walt, and my friend Linda Holden for reading early drafts of this novel and giving honest evaluations. I hope you folks like the final product.

Jeanie Fermon, friend and mentor, has my profound personal and professional respect. Jeanie, your quiet elegant manner and interest in me as a person, not just an employee, meant more than I can articulate. I strive to be a class act; granted I often fail; but you inspire me to keep trying. If I ever attain one-half the class you have, I will consider myself successful in that respect. You and I know what your contributions were and how grateful I am to you.

Last, but not least, special thanks go to my dear friend Bonnie Murray. Wow! BJ, we have both come a long way from our days of creating Call Management Training scripts and putting together those "BJ and Boop training sessions" at good ole HP. Thanks for sharing 50 years of friendship with me; life has been quite a trip for you and I so far, hasn't it? Shall we try for 50 more?

PROLOGUE

"Watch out you crazy nigger; you're gonna kill yourself."

Jo's head snaps up; her stomach muscles tense; the hair on the back of her neck stands up. She experiences, once again, the almost forgotten sensation of panic that occurs each time she hears that word.

A glance out the window reveals two grinning African-American youngsters zigzagging down the sidewalk on skateboards. Jo realizes that the young boys are teasing each other; their grins make it oblivious that they are comfortable using that word. Jo knows that her reaction to the innocent teasing of two young boys is ridicules; but she is helpless to shrug off her discomfort and get on with her day. Her mental floodgates are wide open and she is awash in memories from her early childhood in South Alabama. After a brief attempt to stop the memories, she gives up and just allows them to flow, unchecked.

She can still feel the sting of the slap across her face that her mother gave her immediately following her first utterance of that word – Nigger. She can still see the annoyed glint in her mother's narrowed eyes and hear the steely anger in her voice as she admonishes, "Don't you ever let me hear you say that word again."

Over the years, Jo encountered that word many times; she even uttered it a few times, when she was sure that neither of her parents was within hearing range.

Her thoughts returned to the present and she became aware that her stomach was queasy and her hands were clammy. She admonished herself: "Oh for land's sake, it's just a word, worse than a lot of words, not as bad as some. Why do I continue to react so strongly to it after all these years?"

Jo continues to sit on her porch watching the sunset fade and musing upon the South of her childhood.

Ah, the South, what a complex, enchanting and confusing part of the world - home to an array of races, religions and cultures - a place where slow talkin' folks are slow to change their customs. A land and state of mind that that can't be fully understood or appreciated unless you have lived it - a mixture of things wonderful and things evil; sometimes very evil.

Until late in the 1940's most folks in the South seldom questioned segregation. It caused frustration, aggravation, and inconvenience, but for the most part, it was accepted as just 'the way things are down here'. A few whites, including Jo's father, worked quietly to eliminate or change some of the cruel elements of segregation but, mostly, even these fair-minded folks, didn't raise much ruckus.

In the 1950's a whole lot of Southerners, white and black, lose their naivety and began to reevaluate many of their beliefs about the Southern way of life. Jo, a teenager at the time, was certain that things were going to change drastically and she had a premonition that things were likely to get worse, much worse, before they got better.

To this day, Jo often picks up a newspaper or magazine, and reads some writers distorted image of the South - a South, populated entirely by poor, sad, downtrodden blacks and mean spirited, bullying whites. Oh yes, there were plenty of poor, sad, downtrodden blacks, as well as, a more than ample supply of mean spirited, bullying whites in the old South. The old South -

the pre 1950's era - was also home to many loving, peaceful folks of both races who enjoyed the good thing about their way of life, put up with the bad, and managed to respect and co-exist with each other in relative harmony.

Jo was a perceptive child, acutely aware of injustices of segregation and of the need for these things to change. Yet, she instinctively knew that the manner in which civil rights advocates were trying to force the South to change would bring out the "red neck" stubbornness that some Southerners possessed. Plenty of Southern white folks were disgusted by the way black folks were treated; indeed some white folks were working, in their own slow moving, low key way to change things; but, when confronted by 'pushy civil rights Yankees', these folks completely rejected their suggestions. Some not only ceased their efforts to change things, they aligned themselves with the segregationist and began actively opposing integration.

At times, Jo missed the South of her childhood; it was a good place for a child to inhabit; life was simpler there before she heard of 'civil rights' - before a young black woman had tried to integrate the University of Alabama. Most of all life was simpler before her beloved Daddy felt compelled to tangle with union bosses and the Klan over the treatment of black employees in the paper manufacturing business.

> Sadly, those things had happened, and she couldn't erase the memory of them any more than she could stop her reaction to that word. No, not just that word, a whole damn group of words - Nigger, Colored, Negro, Black, "The Blacks", Black Folks. She hated the way these WORDS seemed to take on a life of their own and become more important than deeds to otherwise rational, intelligent people.

CHAPTER 1

Daddy's Dead

One glance at Sarah Simmons face revealed that, she had endured a sleepless night. Her pretty, olive skinned complexion is wan, her eyes are puffy, and her lips drawn up into a thin line of displeasure. Her husband didn't come home last night and she spent the long lonely hours alternating between worry and anger. Right now, she is angry and doesn't much care that her father-in-law has been seriously ill or that for the past two weeks; her husband has spent part of each evening helping his mother care for his ailing father. To Sarah's way of thinking, there simply was no excuse for her husband's failure to come home to her and her girls.

Sarah heard the back gate slam; she rushed to the kitchen door, and jerked it open just as her husband approached the steps. "It's about time you remembered to come home to me and your daughters, Raymond Archibald Simmons."

"Not now, Sarah; I'm not up to arguin' with you."

Ray's brown eyes lack their usual warmth; his hair, normally slicked back with Fitch's Brilliantine, is disheveled. His broad shoulders are slumped, and he looks utterly drained. He brushes passed Sarah, collapses into a kitchen chair with a deep sigh. "Daddy's dead and it's my fault."

"Lord have mercy on his soul and grant him eternal peace." Sarah's voice is now soft and comforting, with all traces of anger gone. "I'm so sorry. How can you possibly think his death is in any way your fault? Your Daddy has been ailin' for over two weeks and you've been practically livin' at your folks; helpin' your Momma nurse him."

"That's all I knew to do, but I tell you, it wasn't nearly enough."

A hint of anger crept back into Sarah's voice. "You've been over there way more than the others; he was their father too; it seems like y'all could've divided nursin' him a little more evenly."

"Damn it, Sarah! Don't start."

"I'm just tryin' to figure out why you think it's your fault that your Daddy died."

"Oh! All right! You not gonna give me a minutes peace 'til I talk about it, are you?"   Ray wearily gets up and begins to pace. "Daddy's been in real bad shape for the last few days. The doctor said he had developed pneumonia. He was runnin' a high fever and coughin' so bad that he could hardly catch his breath; but he kept insistin' that he was gettin' better - I knew he really wasn't - but he made Momma promise not to let anybody take him to the hospital and I couldn't budge her from that promise. Hell, he even got old Doc Hawthorne on his side; Doc told us that we could nurse him at home just as well as they could at the hospital. I knew better; I should've stood up to Momma and Doc; Daddy needed to be in the Le Grand Infirmary where they have oxygen tents and stuff for pneumonia patients; if he'd been there he probably would have pulled through."

Sarah walked over to Ray and put her arms around him. "You don't know that. You can't tell how it's gonna' come out with pneumonia; some folks get over it just fine and other, seemingly strong folks, just cannot shake it off. It's Gods will and that's all there is to it."

"Could you just put on a pot of coffee, please?" Ray shrugs away from her. "Soon as I rest a minute, I'm gonna go take a shower and try to pull myself together."

Sarah, hurt that Ray rejected her attempt to hug him, walks away and begins preparing the coffee. As she measures the coffee grounds, she asks; "Were any of the others with him at the end?"

"Just me and Momma."

"Soon as I get this coffee goin', I'll run over and tell Lilly Ann about ya'll's Daddy passin'.""

"I stopped in at her place on the way home; she's gonna go down to Wilton's place and drive him and Bessie over to

Momma's. Then, she's goin' to get Betty Sue and Bobby.   I stopped in at Donny's place for a minute, too."

"Seems like you weren't in any hurry to come home; guess you didn't care that I was worried sick picturin' you dead or hurt on the side of the road or lost somewhere out in that short cut through the paper-mill woods."

"Damn it, don't fuss at me; I only stopped long enough to ask if I could use his pickup to run up to Centerville to bring Daddy's kin down from the loggin camp. He said I should stay down here with Momma and y'all. He's gonna run up there and fetch 'em; he's a good friend and I'm beholden to him."

"Maybe, I should ride along with Lilly Ann."

"I'm sure she's gone already; we're gonna meet all of 'em over at Momma's; we've gotta make funeral arrangements."

"Well, I'll take the girls out for a walk and let you get a little rest before you head back over there."

"There's not time for that; you're gonna have to wait awhile before you start runnin' the streets and gettin' sympathy from all your friends. Just pack the stuff we need, and get yourself and the girls ready to go over to Momma's; I don't want her alone right now. I told her I'd bring y'all back as soon as I could."

"Seems like you left her alone to come get us; so, a few more minutes won't matter."

"Damn it! Stop! I need you with me on this. Miz Velma is over at Momma's right now, but she's gonna have to go and tend her cows pretty soon and I want to be get back to Momma's before then."

"I reckon Miz Velma's cows can wait 'til Lilly Ann gets Wilton and Bessie over there."

"Go or stay; right now I don't give a damn. I'm goin' to Momma's and I'm goin as quick as I can. If you're not goin', get the girls' stuff together, 'cause I'm takin' them with me."

Sarah bit back a retort as she slammed the coffee pot on the burner, spun on her heels, left the kitchen, and reluctantly begun preparing to go with Ray.

Sara's emotions are in turmoil. She has a great deal of affection for her mother-in-law and wants to comfort her. Nonetheless, hates spending time with Ray's siblings. Whenever, these siblings are together, their affection and delight in each others company takes over and they often forget to include Sarah in their strolls down memory lane - she resents this. Sarah's self-esteem is fragile; she craves the lime light, because it feeds her ego and reassures her, she is important. When others focus their attention elsewhere, Sarah pouts.

As Sarah packs, she has a strange premonition that her father-in-law's death is going to cause things to change drastically for her, Ray and the girls; she hopes against hope that the feeling is wrong; she likes her life just fine and doesn't want to change a thing.

Ray quickly showers, drinks his coffee, and goes into the front room where Sarah has just finished dressing the girls.

"Are you about ready?"

"As ready as I'm gonna be."

Sarah has packed a small suitcase and loaded the stroller with diapers, bottles, and other things she will need for the girls. Ray picks up Margaret Ann, his shy, dark haired three-year-old daughter, and the small suitcase; Sarah picks up the baby, Nancy

Josephine, and nestles the chubby cheeked infant among the things in the stroller. Reluctantly Sarah opens the door and walks out onto the front porch, thinking, "I wish I could just stay home today, doll up my pretty girls, stroll to town and shop; maybe, just maybe, if I don't go to North Le Grand nothing will have to change for Ray and me." For a moment, she is afraid that she actually spoke her thought aloud. A quick glance at Ray assures her that she hadn't done so.

Sarah knows that her place is with her husband's family during this time of loss and she forces herself to continue down the steps and across the yard. At the edge of the lawn, she stops, closes her eyes, breathes the fresh morning air; the slightly marshy aroma produced by the muddy ground and decaying vegetation along the banks of Indian River which is just east of town. It has a wide deep-water channel that empties into the mouth of Le Grand Bay; and is ideally suited for the large shipbuilding and repair facility located on its west bank.

In the early 1920's employees of the shipbuilding company were threatening to leave the company unless their living conditions were improved. Therefore, the company replaced the tent city that had sprung up on the riverbank. Rather than build an ordinary "mill village"; like the ones that workers at local paper mills and saw mills developed; they built an entire town. It was a well-planned community with attractive and well-built homes, wide streets, a municipal golf course, a sewage disposal plant and a small business district. They named the town Indian Grove.

"Come on, Mama's waitin' for us." Ray urges; and with a sad little sigh, Sarah begins moving again. They pass the municipal golf course and proceed along the wide tree lined sidewalks of the residential section

As they leave the residential area, Ray instinctively turns south toward the paper mill

"Where do you think you're goin'?" Sarah demands.

Ray stops, shakes his head, and flashes Sarah a very brief smile; "Sorry, "I'm not thinkin' straight this mornin'; I forgot I'm not goin' to work today."   For the past three years, Ray has worked, as a laborer, at the paper mill south of Indian Grove.

He changed direction headed toward the Indian Grove business district.   It isn't much; just a three block cluster of buildings along a strip of Highway 43, north of where Telegraph Road and Craft Highway intersect. Here, merchants and service providers have rented the stores and business places from the ship building company and a United States Post Office has been given one of the buildings so that Indian Grove and the adjacent area has mail delivery service.

One side of the street has a drug store/soda fountain, a dry goods store, Delchamps Grocery, the post office, and a doctor's office; the other houses an auto repair shop/filling station, a produce stand and an elementary school. When the family reaches the school, Sarah slows a moment to admire the magnificent bronze statue on the lawn - a replica of an Indian Chief astride a horse; he is wearing a feathered headdress, has his head thrown back and his arms lifted to the heavens.

As they enter the rural area of North Le Grande, Sarah becomes acutely aware of its contrast to Indian Grove. North Le Grande has unpaved, red clay roads that are dusty during dry weather and became sticky red mud when it rains. The right of way, for these narrow roads is lined with rows of rural mailboxes and, of course, there are no sidewalks. The landscape is dotted with small, mostly unpainted, wooden frame houses that have no electricity, no gas, no indoor plumbing. Folks in North Le Grand get their light from kerosene lamps; cook on kerosene or coal burning stoves; keep warm with 'potbellied' stoves or kerosene heaters; get water from pumps on the back porch or in the back yard and when nature calls, they use outhouses or 'privies', by day, and chamber pots at night. Most folks keep their perishables in 'iceboxes' that are cooled by 25 or 50-pound blocks of ice. These blocks of ice are delivered by the "ice wagon", a couple of times a week.

Nothing out here appeals to Sarah; she heaves a sigh and mutters, softly so that Ray won't hear, "Whoever named this area was surely a jokester; there's nothing grand about North Le Grande."

CHAPTER 2

The Family Gathers

Sarah and her mother-in-law have little in common; nonetheless, since Ray and Sarah's marriage, they have come to care deeply for each other. As soon as she sees her mother-in-law, Sarah perceives that something is vastly different about her, but she can't quite put her finger on what the difference is.

Miz Simmons is usually clad in one of the plain cotton dresses, which she makes on the Singer sewing machine that her husband gave her when she was a young bride. When she works in her vegetable garden, she wears a smock over her dress and a wide brimmed sunbonnet; when she is in the kitchen, fixin' supper or puttin' up vegetables for winter, she wears a large bib apron over her dress. True, it seems strange, in the middle of the week, for Miz Simmons to be wearing a Sunday-go-to-meeting, 'store bought' dress with a small frilly apron tied around her trim waist. However, Sara knows there is more than that difference - something that goes much deeper than her mother-in-law's manner of dress. Then, like a bolt out of the blue, Sarah realizes it's the eyes; Miz Simmons eyes are dull and flat, as though someone has turned off a light deep in her soul. Seeing the older woman looking so devastated tugs at Sarah's heart, she fights back a sob as they affectionately embraced each other.

"I'm so sorry; I just don't know what I would do if I were in your shoes; please tell me what I can do to help you."

"Just let me hug the girls. Then, come sit in the kitchen and keep me company while I make some breakfast for all of us."

"Now, Miz Simmons, you don't need to be cookin' and doin' chores at a time like this; let me get breakfast started; when Lilly Ann and the rest of 'em get here, we'll take care of anything else that needs doin'."

"No, I can't sit around and let y'all wait on me; I know that the Good Lord will get me through this, but I need to keep my hands and my mind busy until I figure out just how he's plannin' to do it."

"OK, if that's what you want. Just let me know if you change your mind."

The Simmons family is still sitting at the breakfast table when friends and neighbors begin arriving with dishes of food, condolences, and offers to help in anyway that is needed.

Lilly Ann, being the oldest of the Simmons siblings, takes on the chore of organizing things.

"Ray, since you and Momma aren't eatin' a thing anyway, y'all go into the front parlor and sit with the folks that are comin' in. When the rest of us finish breakfast, Wilton and Wayne can go tend the chickens and round up extra chairs for the parlor. Sarah as soon as your done eatin', corral all the kids in the big back bedroom and keep them out from under foot; Bessie can start washin' the breakfast dishes; and Betty Sue and I will make room in the ice box and on the side board for all this food that folks are bringin'."

Sarah glares at Lilly Ann, throws down her napkin, shifts Jo from her lap to her hip, grabs Margaret Ann by the hand, and flounces from the kitchen. As she passes Lily Ann's chair she mutters, just loudly enough for everyone to hear: "Well! Well! Miss Lilly Ann has spoken, so I guess I know my place. I'd better get on in the back bedroom where y'all can ignore me. Y'all just send the other kids on in when they're done eatin'."

Ray flushes a bright red, as he helps his mother from her chair; Lilly Ann gives his shoulder a pat and pretends not to hear the sarcasm in her sister-in-law's voice; the others keep their eyes on their plates and continue eating.

Ray speaks a few words to the friends and relatives as they arrive; other than that, he sits stone-faced, silent, and dry eyed by his mother's side. By mid afternoon, Miz Simmons can tell that her youngest son is on the verge of exhaustion. "You need to go and get a little rest."

"I'm fine. I don't want to leave you."

"Now you listen, Ray, your daddy is expectin' you to help carry his casket to its final restin' place, and if you don't get a little rest, I'm afraid you may pass out and fall flat on your face while doin' it. Go on, now; do like I tell you; Lilly Ann can sit with me and help greet folks. I'll be fine."

Reluctantly Ray leaves his mother's side; he stops in the kitchen to talk to Lilly Ann; he eats the pie and coffee that some thoughtful neighbor places in front of him; he wanders into the back bedroom to check on Sarah and his daughters. Sarah can see how exhausted he is; she feels guilty about her earlier outburst and attempts to make up for it.

"Honey, you look worn out; why don't you grab a nap before the rest of your kin get here?"

"Momma needs me, I'll take a walk out back to stretch my legs a little bit; then, get back to Momma."

"Margaret Ann hasn't seen much of you today. She doesn't really understand what's happenin' and she has missed you. Lay there on the day bed and snuggle her a bit. It'll do both of you good."

"OK, I'll rest my eyes a minute while I hold her; then, I'm goin' right back to Momma."

Ray stretches out and promptly falls asleep. About an hour later, he wakes to find Margaret Ann curled up beside him, humming softly. He tweaked her nose and smiled; "I reckon, we were both pooped - that nap felt good, didn't it?" Margaret Ann grinned and buried her head in the crook of his arm.

After giving his daughter one last squeeze, Ray rises, gives Sarah a gentle hug, a quick kiss and heads out to the kitchen There he finds Lilly Ann is making sandwiches. "Want one of these?" She asks.

"Nope, I've gotta get back to Momma."

"You might want to take a short detour; Mema and the folks from Centerville came in while you were restin'; she's out back; why don't you go to her."

"Thanks."

Ray goes to find his grandmother, the tiny Cherokee woman whose teachings have so influenced his life, and who he loves almost beyond reason. He spots her, sitting very straight and stiff on a hard wooden chair beside the feed shed; his eyes fill with tears; he rushes to her. "Oh! Mema! I'm so sorry". He crumples at her feet, puts his head in her lap, and sobs out his anguish. His grandmother sits, gently stroking his head, until the storm of his sobs subside. When he raises his head, she sees the torment in his eyes. "Boy, what is it that's troubling your spirit so; you're hurting way beyond what your daddy's passing accounts for."

"I could have saved him and I didn't."

"That's rubbish, boy. You explain yourself right now!"

"He didn't want to go to the hospital; but he needed to be there. If I had ignored his request and taken him to Le Grand Infirmary, he would still be alive"

"Hog wash; you know better! The time a man dies is up to the Great Spirit; haven't I taught you since you were a young child that no man goes before his time?"

"Yes, but hospitals have things, like oxygen tents, that could have saved him."

"Not if the Great Spirit wanted otherwise. I'm glad that you didn't deny your father his last wish; the time and place of his passing was between him and his maker and you were right not to interfere."

"I'm not so sure, but hearin' you say so has lifted my spirit and eased my mind a little."

"Don't sass me. I know what I'm sayin' is true, and don't you dare act like it ain't. We've got some more talkin' to do; so, let's walk while we do it. I need to get the travel kinks out of these old bones."

She rises, taking Ray's arm to steady herself. They walk in silence for a few minutes. Finally, she begins speaking; "This isn't easy for me to say; my son turned away from his kin, let his way of thinkin' get clouded, took up with folks that he shouldn't have paid any mind to; he adopted their bigoted, intolerant, and uncaring ways; even toward his own people. Do you know what I'm talking about, or do I have to spell it out for you?"

"I know, Mema."

"For a long time now my mind has been troubled; I mourn that, he grew away from me and rejected my teaching. I'm saddened by the fact that we quarreled these last few years.

Somehow, I couldn't seem to reach him and change his way of thinking. Pay attention to what I'm saying, I don't want to lose you that way. Do you hear me?"

"You aren't gonna lose me; I'll bring Momma, Sarah and the girls to see you often and you can come and stay with us some." "

"That's a promise that I hope you keep; but, I'm talking about more than just visiting."

"What is it that you want of me?"

"You're like your father in many ways; he was a good man and so are you. You've always been taught to protect your family, but I want your promise that you won't travel down your daddy's road and make the same mistakes he did. In his mind, he was protecting y'all by getting' mixed up with the Klan, but we both know that wasn't so. Stay true to your beliefs, even when it seems like you're putting those you love in harms way. No good can come of rejectin' your heritage."

"You don't need to worry, Mema. I've got a couple of reasons for stayin' away from the Klan; most important, I know how it would hurt you if I took up with their kind. Daddy was ponderin' what to do about them when he died. A few months ago, Daddy and me had a long talk. He said it shamed him to be hidin' his Indian blood; said he had come to disagree with what the Klan was doin' and rued the day he got in with them. I asked him why he didn't get out. He shook his head, said it wasn't that simple, and walked off."

"If hiding his blood shamed him, then he didn't fully reject my people; that is a comfort to me. You've seen with your own eyes how white folks judge the Cherokee; you've seen, too, how some of the Cherokee turned on me for marrying a white man. All that judgin' and blamin' caused my son a great deal of pain as he was growing up; maybe that's what caused him to go to judgin' others so harshly."

"I don't know, Mema."

"Promise me that you won't give in to the temptation to judge any man before you get to know him; promise, too, that you won't flaunt or deny your roots."

"I give you my solemn promise; I'll heed your words."

"You're a good boy; now let's go home and bury our dead."

CHAPTER 3

Movin' to North Le Grand

A few day after the burying their father, Ray and his siblings are sitting around the kitchen table discussing what to do about their mother.

"I don't like the idea of Momma out here all by herself; do y'all?" Ray offers.

Wilton vows, "No way am I gonna' let her stay here without Daddy. My house is small, and we're pretty crowded, what with Bessie's momma livin' with us; but I can always make room for more kin if I need to."

Betty Sue enters the discussion, "No need for that, Bob and I can stay out here with her for awhile. We have been talkin' about gettin' a bigger place; the baby is about to out grow her crib and there's no way we can fit a single bed in that little alcove where she's sleepin' now. Bob doesn't like it out here very much, but he can adjust as long as he knows it ain't gonna be forever."

"No! Mama can crowd in with us until our new house is done; its already more than half built and when we move in there we're gonna have plenty of room." "Anyway", Lilly Ann declares, "I'm the oldest and she should live with me."

Miz Simmons walks in, casts a stern look around the room, and shocks her grown-up children by announcing; "I'm neither deaf nor addle brained; in case y'all forgot, I've been sittin' right out there on that porch listenin' to y'all squabble like kindergarteners fightin over who gets the red crayon. 'I want Momma.' – 'No! She is better off with me' - 'No! I said so first.' - 'But I'm the oldest." Y'all act like this pore old woman can't think for herself and y'all are in charge. Ain't none of it gonna' happen! Thank you very much, but I'll take care of myself right here in the house that my husband built for me and I don't need nobody livin' with me while I do it either; end of discussion."

"But Momma."

"No buts about it; my mind's made up. I hope y'all come visit often, cause I know I'm gonna be lonely, but, be that as it may, I have no intention of leavin' my home or havin' any of y'all leave yours."

Late in the afternoon, Ray and Wilton walk out back for a smoke; once they're well out of earshot of their mother, Ray reveals his plan. "I don't know why I didn't think of this before now. Take a good look over there." Ray points to the house next door. "You know Daddy's death was such a shock that I forgot all about my place; Daddy and I got it all boxed in, put the roof on and were makin' good progress with the inside work when he took sick. Hell, it's livable right now; I'm gonna move me, Sarah and the girls on out here right away and do the finish work after we get settled. If Momma puts up a squawk, I'll just tell her that, without Daddy to help me, the rest of the work will go quicker if we live out here. I don't see how she can object to that, do you?"

"No, Momma won't object, but you better talk it over with Sarah before you get your heart set on it."

"No need to, I'm just pushin' the schedule up a little; we've been plannin' to live out here as soon as the house was finished."

"Yeah, I know that's what you and Daddy figured; but, I suspect that Sarah has a different idea. Good luck, getting' her to leave Indian Grove."

"Aw, she'll be fine out here; she's always braggin' to anybody who'll listen about us havin' a home out in the country."

"Well, I know Sarah likes braggin', but if you pay close attention, she always brags that y'all have a 'vacation' home out in the county, and that's a darn sight different than livin' out here all the time. I tell you Sarah ain't a country girl and she ain't gonna' like leavin' town to live in the sticks."

Ray discovers just how right Wilton was about Sarah not being a country girl. When he brought up the subject of moving to Le Grand, Sarah's reaction was totally negative; this flabbergasts him. "What wrong with you? We've talked about this lots of times; how come all the sudden you are so set against it?'

Sarah clinches her teeth and glares; "There's nothin' wrong with me. You are being ridicules. That was just talk; I never meant we'd move as soon as the house was finished; just maybe later, - much later."

"Oh bologna, Sarah, I'm not buying any of that crap. How dumb do you think I am? You acted like you were all for movin' out here."

"That's not so; the only time I talked about it is when you pushed me into a corner. Name me one time when I brought up the subject - you can't - it was always you - you wantin' to live out here where the girls could get lots of fresh air and we could put down roots; and; me just goin' along until I figured a way to change your mind."

"You're lyin', I never pushed you; you tricked me into thinkin' you wanted the same thing I did."

"You may want to live way out there in the sticks, but NOT ME. If I ever live there, it won't be 'til I'm old and gray and the darned place has built up so there are more things to do."

"Hell, woman, you kept insistin' on changes in the design, even after Daddy and I started buildin'. Why on earth would you do that if you had no plans to live in it?"

"I really didn't give it much though; I just liked havin' somethin' to say when Lilly Ann was braggin' about all the stuff she was havin' put in her new house. Anyhow, I can 'think about it' until the cows come home and it won't change anything; I don't want to live there."

"Damn it! I work for what we've got, and you know I don't give a damn about tryin' to keep up with what Lilly Ann and Wayne do. You can't expect me to keep payin' rent when we own a perfectly good house."

"Why not? If you really want me and the girls to be happy, you will."

Realizing that Sarah is angry to the point of becoming irrational, Ray announces. "Look, I'm fed up with arguin', I've got to be at work early in the mornin' so I'm goin' to bed; we'll talk when I get home from work tomorrow." Ray stalks off to the bedroom, and slams the door.

Sarah pours herself a glass of iced tea and walks out to the front porch to drink it and let her temper cool down some. Unfortunately, she can't stop thinking about North Le Grand and she gets angrier by the minute as she mentally ticks off what life out there is like. "No electricity! Oh Lord, I'll have to give up my radio and record player, NO - I can't stand that. I'll go crazy if I can't play the Victrola and listen to my records. The new Frigidaire - it took me almost a year to talk the landlord into buying it for us; how can Ray expect me to give that up and use one of those horrid iceboxes? No indoor plumbing! No more long hot soaks in the big bathtub. Just thinkin' about haulin' in the washtub and pumpin' enough water for a bath makes me tired. Heaven help me; I can't use an outhouse all the time; it's bad enough usin' one when we visit Miz Simmons."

Around midnight Sarah becomes determined that she isn't leaving Indian Grove; she calms herself down, and begins concocting schemes to bring Ray around to her way point of view.   She considers and discards half a dozen schemes to accomplish this; finally, a bit after two o'clock in the morning, she crawls into bed, snuggles up to Ray's back, and goes to sleep.

As soon as Ray is out the door, headed for the paper-mill, she springs into action. Before her daughters wake up, she takes a bath and puts her hair up in rollers. When her daughters awake, she feeds, bathes, and dresses them, and they head for town. Under normal circumstances, she wouldn't dream of being seen in town with a head full of rollers covered by a scarf; but, this wasn't normal circumstances; besides, she had little time to worry about what her friends would think, she was on a mission of great importance.

First stop is the Dry Goods store to see if they have gotten in that new Bing Crosby record that Ray has been wanting - she is in luck, they have it. On to Delchamps where she heads to the butcher counter in the back of the store.

"Mornin' Miz Sarah, how are you and those pretty little ones doin' today?"

"Just fine, Mr. Leon, and you?"

"Couldn't be better."

"I really need one of your best beef rib roasts; you know the kind Ray likes best; make it about four pounds; that way I'll have meat left over to pack in tomorrow's lunch for him."

"OK, Sarah, I'll get right on it; won't be more than a few minutes."

"Don't rush, the girls and I have to shop for the rest of the supper and desert fixins."

Shopping completed. Sara loads her purchases in the baby carriage with Jo and starts walking home. On an impulse, she stops by the filling station and gets six bottles of the beer that Ray prefers to drink.

Sarah spends the afternoon cleaning, cooking, and primping.

That evening, Ray walks into a serene home; the aroma of roasting beef fills his nostrils; the sound of Bing Crosby fills his ears; and the coup de grace is the sight of Sarah, Margaret Ann, Jo, and the kitchen each cleaned and polished to a fare-thee-well.

"Wow, are we expecting company?" Ray wants to know.

"Of course not." Sarah gives him a hug and speaks in a soft breathy voice. She is working her plan as hard as she can; "I just think you need a little cheering up. Losing your father hit you pretty hard".

She hands him the baby, flashes him a smile, goes to the Fridigaire, gets him a cold beer, kisses him on the cheek, and tells him to relax and enjoy his beer and his children until supper is ready.

Ray tries not to be suspicious of Sarah's sudden spurt of domestic activity and her good mood; but he can't shake the feeling that she is trying to soften him up. He hopes that the proposed move to North Le Grand is not at the root of her attempts.

He casually interjects the subject of the move into their after supper conversation. Instead of getting upset and yelling, Sarah puts phase two of her plan into action; she begins crying, wringing her hands, looking as forlorn as the heroine in a Greek tragedy, and speaking in a trembling little voice. "I know you work hard for our money, but I really don't want to move. Maybe we can rent out the house in North Le Grande and make enough money to cover the rent here. I just can't live out in the sticks."

"Be logical, it doesn't make sense to rent out a brand new house, one that we own free and clear by the way; what's more that would do nothing to solve the situation of Momma being out there alone."

Sensing that her theatrics were not having the desired effect, Sarah let her anger show again.

"Why does it have to be us livin out there? You have three siblings, in case you forgot; one of them can darned well move out there if they are of a mind to. I have no intention of livin' out there - never did."

"That's news to me; you never said anything about not wantin' to live out there while Daddy and I were bustin' our butts to build the place."

'I don't care what you say; I'm not leavin' Indian Grove."

"It's settled! Damn it! I'm movin' out there and I'm takin' the girls with me. If you choose not to accompany me, that's your business. You can stay here, but you're gonna' have to figure out how we can afford two places, 'cause I'm only supportin' one."

Sarah knows she is losing the battle, so she switches tactics, again. "Oh Ray, honey", she practically coos as she fluffs her hair, "can't we stay here 'til the girls are a little older? Margaret Ann is too little to walk very far and I can't push Jo's stroller on those old dirt roads out there. I'll go nuts stranded out there all day with two little kids. It's just too far from all the things the girls and I enjoy."

Ray's reply is short and to the point. "No!" He wants no more of Sarah's theatrics; he grabs another beer from the Frigidaire, and heads out to the front porch.

"You can't do this to me." Sarah wails as she runs after him, trailing crocodile tears in her wake. He ignores her and after a couple of minutes she retreats into the house and slams the door to make sure Ray knows that she is still mad.

In a matter of weeks, Ray moves to North Le Grande, and a reluctant Sarah goes with him.

Ray tries to appease Sarah and make things in North Le Grand more appealing to her. His first project is to add two huge rooms to the house - one on each end of their large front porch.

He encloses the top half of each room with screen wire, to catch the evening breezes and achieve better ventilation. He dubs one of the rooms the *sleepin' porch* because he and Sarah plan to sleep there during the hot summer months.

Tongue in cheek, he dubs the other room the drawin' room and sets up his mechanical drawing equipment there. Mechanical drawing is one of Ray's passions; he learned the basics in high school, discovered that he had a real talent for it, and continued to perfect his skill over the years since graduation.

CHAPTER 4

A Son Is Born

Shortly after moving to North Le Grande, Sarah becomes pregnant.

Her first two pregnancies had been easy; she felt good most of the time, and loved the attention that Ray and her friends showered on her. This pregnancy, however, is very different; most days her morning sickness is more like all day sickness and she is racked by nausea until late afternoon. Her feet and hands swell; she tires easily and cries for no apparent reason. Taking care of her home and daughters in an acceptable manner is beyond her ability. She welcomes the help and companionship of her mother-in-law and Miz Velma; but she also, misses the bustle of life in Indian Grove and resents not having the conveniences that she enjoyed when she lived there. She is upset and disappointed to learn that she will not be able to deliver her third child at home, as she did with both of her daughters. Her doctor, fearing unpredictable complications, insists that she give birth in a hospital.

As dawn is breaking, on a chilly spring morning, Sarah waked Ray, "Its time for us to go. You have to wake up now."

"The sun's not up yet; I don't have to go to work this early." Ray mumbles.

"You're not goin' to work, now get up."

"Is it Saturday?"

"No, idiot, I'm havin' your baby."

The last remark cut through the sleepy fog in Ray's mind and he jumped out of the bed like a scalded cat. He shoved his feet into his slippers, grabbed the suitcase that Sarah had ready at the end of the bed, and headed out the door, yelling over his shoulder, "I'll go warm the car while you get your bathrobe on."

"Hold on, Come back here, put on some pants, go get your mother to come over here so she can watch the girls and help me get ready to go; then, you can go warm the car."

"OK, I'm really awake now. You relax; I'll take care of everything and get you to the hospital in one piece."

Following a long difficult labor, Sarah gives birth to a healthy, husky, brown-eyed baby boy with a dimple in each cheek and pale blonde fuzz covering his head. She names the baby Carrington Archibald; Carrington is Sarah's maiden sir name; and Archibald, to honor his father.

Ray is surprised and frustrated to find that the hospital allows him very limited access to his newborn son. Since his daughters had been birthed at home, he had enjoyed unlimited access to them almost from the moment of their birth; thus, he is elated when the hospital releases Sarah and the baby.

When they arrive home, Ray leaves Sarah in the capable hands of his mother and takes his son out to the drawin' room, to get acquainted with him. Ray sits down in a rocking chair, removes the blanket and examines the baby from head to toe.

When he is satisfied that nothing is amiss, he rewraps the blanket; then, holding his infant son in his arms, he begins to rock and speak softly to him.

"Carrington Archibald Simmons, your romantic mother has given you a rather fancy name; I can tell you right now that nobody in this family is gonna call you all those names, so how 'bout if you and I decide what you'll be called."

The baby makes a nuzzling move and pushes his head closer to his daddy's chest. "I'm glad you agree with me. Now let's see, maybe we could use just your initials, C-A-S, and call you Cas … um … Cas … Yep, that sounds pretty good to me."

The infant squirms and whimpers. "Oh, you don't like it; why is that?"

Ray puts the baby up on his shoulder and rubs his back to sooth him. "Hum … oh … I see. You're worried about what the schoolyard bullies can do with it. Well, OK. Let's think about that a littler bit."

Ray rocks and muses, "Yes, they could chant 'Cas, Cas green as grass, sitting on his big fat ...' OOPS. You're right, that'll never do."

Ray hums softly as he continues to think of what to call his son. "Well, you can't be called Archie because a couple of my great aunts call me that and we don't want to confuse elderly ladies by having two of us called Archie, do we? How about, we just shorten up Carrington and make it Cary?"

Ray looks down at his son and is sure he sees the baby smile. "Well , OK, then, I can see that you like that one, it's a good sounding' name and the bullies can't do much with it. Well, maybe they could say, 'Cary me back to Ole Virginie' but that's a wimpy insult. Besides, in my experience, bullies usually aren't into music, so they probably won't even think of that - Cary it will be. Welcome home Cary. It's gonna be nice having another male around here."

Sarah's health remains poor after Cary is born; she is weak, tires easily, and shows very little interest in Ray, her children or her home. Miz Simmons tries to shoulder Sarah's household and childcare responsibilities, but within a few weeks of Cary's birth, it became apparent that she simply couldn't continue to manage two households, so Ray hires Miz Velma.

Miz Velma is shirttail kin, her alcoholic husband is the brother of Ray's sister-in-law, Bessie; Ray has known Miz Velma since he was a teenager. She is a warm and loving woman, a wonderful cook and an excellent homemaker; she has an ample bosom and a wide comfortable lap that is perfect for comforting babies and small children. Miz Velma's greatest sadness is not having any of her own. During Sarah pregnancy, Miz Velma encouraged Margaret Ann and Jo to spend time at her house, so their mother could rest. She loved having them visit with her while she milked her cows and churned butter. Now she delights in caring for them and the new baby. Cary and Miz Velma immediately bond and that bond is indestructible; it endures until her death - many years in the future. She accepts Ray's payment for her services only because her husband seldom has a job, and when he does, he drinks up most of his pay, so she really needs the money.

About two years after Ray and Sarah move to North Le Grande, the county extends electricity and city water lines out to that area. Ray installs two water faucets, one in the kitchen and one in the back yard, and wires the sleepin' porch and his drawin' room for electricity.

Sarah reacts with indifference to these improvements; "Big deal! We still don't have an indoor bathroom or any money to buy what we need to put one in or get us a Frigidaire. I'll probably be dead and buried before things are as nice out here as they were in Indian Grove."

He tries to cheer her up with a trip to the big furniture store in downtown Le Grande. He has her select two comfortable chairs and a new Victrola to put in the sleepin' porch so she can sit and enjoy her music. Unfortunately, even that effort didn't produce any noticeable excitement in her.

Miz Velma had the opposite reaction to having runnin' water; she raves about how wonderful it is.

"I declare Ray, this is just the nicest thing you could have done! I only have to turn the knob to get the kids a drink anytime they are thirsty; I've got all the water I could ever want for cookin' and cleanin', right here at the kitchen sink. Lord be praised, I can even make the kids a bath and never have to make one trip out to the well - just fill the kettle right here at the kitchen sink, put it on the stove, and before long, I've got enough hot water to warm up the tub real nice."

"Aw, it wasn't that much work; it was the least I could do to help y'all out."

You're right about it helping out; it is a whole lot easier to do laundry now that we don't have to haul water from the pump."

"Well, I'm sure glad that you're happy; I think Sarah likes those things too, she just won't admit it because she is still mad at me for movin' out here. The other day I caught her smilin', while she was sittin' in the sleepin' porch listenin' to records on the Victrola. I'm hopin' that she comes out of her funk soon; it's getting real old real fast."

CHAPTER 5

Summer in North Le Grande

Except for her mother-in-law and Miz Velma, Sarah has few friends in the neighborhood. She considers most of her neighbors boring and has little interest in their endless talk of cooking, gardening, cleaning, canning, and sewing; likewise, Sarah's neighbors brand her as lazy and shallow; they don't care for her frivolous chatter about the popular music, movie stars, the latest dance steps, and hairstyles.

One bright spot in Sarah's life is her children; she is somewhat lax in her efforts to groom, feed and educate them, but she loves them fiercely and enjoys their company. With Miz Simmons living on one side, and Miz Zelma living on the other and both of them devoted to Ray and Sarah's kids, the children didn't suffer any ill effects of their mother's neglect of their physical needs.

On summer afternoons, Sarah ignores housework and spends her time sitting on the front porch drinking ice tea, or an RC Cola, and listening to her kids at play. Sarah has only one sibling - a brother; he is much older than she is and they hardly ever played together as children.

The fertile minds and active imaginations of her children amazed her; she never tired of observing their ability to create a world of their own. They loved to pretend that they are sitting in a leafy tree house, somewhere in an Amazon jungle, instead of on the branches of the huge Chinaberry tree in their front yard.

Sometimes Sarah can't resist the urge to become part of the children's play and surprise them with a treat. One of her favorite ways of doing this is to get up from her chair on the porch, wander around the yard, pretending to be interested in the flowerbeds, until she is directly under the Chinaberry tree; then, she places her hands on her hips, and glances up at the kids, "I don't reckon anybody up there wants some fudge."

"I do! I do! I do!" The kids yell in unison as they jump down and race each other into the kitchen.

Sarah assigns each of the kids a chore. "Cary, you get the can of Hershey's Cocoa Powder out of the cabinet; Jo you get the butter out of the ice box; Margaret Ann you get a cup of cool - not cold - just cool - water, for us to use when we test and see if the candy is cooked enough."

Each kid scampers off to do their assigned chore, Sarah gets the stove going, assembles the candy making utensils and ingredients, and the adventure of making candy is off to a good start.

As the candy cooks, the kids stand behind their mother, smelling the wonderful aroma, and wait impatiently for it to be done. When the fudge is cooked, properly tested in the cool - not cold - water, and poured into a buttered platter, Sarah turns to the kids with a mischievous grin; "Anybody want to lick the pan?"

The answer is always the same. "Me! Me! Me!"

Sarah places the warm, but rapidly cooling, pan in the center of the kitchen table, gives each of the kids a spoon and watches as they attack the pan. When they have licked all they can from the pan, she shoos them out to the porch.

"OK, now comes the hard part, we've gotta sit out here and wait until the fudge sets up before we can eat it." It actually takes just a little more than an hour for the fudge to set up, but to the kids it seems to take forever.

Ray's salary at the mill is barely enough to make ends meet. He wants his kids to have more than a hand to mouth type of existence, so he supplements his meager mill income by working part time as a carpenter's helper. When he shows the carpenters some of the house plans that he has drawn, they deem them to be on par with those of many local architects and advise him to continue honing his mechanical drawing skill.

Thus encouraged, he spends many summer evenings working in the drawin' room with the windows open to catch the cooling breeze. Occasionally the sound of his children playing in the chinaberry tree entices him to leave his drawing board, grab a couple of beers, and head out to the front porch. Sometimes he just listens as the kids talk about their activities; other times, he talks to them about his day or tells stories to them.

The kids love their Daddy's stories, especially the stories about his childhood - living with his parents and siblings in logging camps or railroad towns in south Alabama - visiting his maternal grandfather and uncles in Florida and spending time aboard the shrimp boats that they own - caddying at "the links" in Indian Grove.

Jo has a favorite story and each time her Daddy starts reminiscing, she begs for this tale. Ray pretends that he doesn't know which story she wants to hear. "You mean the one about me catchin' a big fish?"

"Not that one Daddy."

"Oh, maybe when Momma caught me skinny dippin' and tanned my hide?"

"No! You know the one I like best."

"Well, how about, when I learned to use a buck saw out in the loggin' camps, is that it?"

Completely exasperated, Jo places her hands on her hips, shakes her head from side to side, stamps her little foot, and gives her Daddy a stern look.

Smothering a grin, Ray rubs his chin and pretends to concentrate; "Oh, I know the one you mean - the one about Lucy givin' me a bath?"

"Yes! That's the one. It's the best story that you tell."

After a long swig of beer, he begins. "When I was a boy of eleven or twelve, Momma hired a nigger washwoman; named Lucy Freeman. I liked Lucy; she told me stories and, kinda like you, I would pester her to tell my favorite one; it was about how she got her name. She would explain how her former master had freed her and her man; how he gave them paying jobs and a place to live. Her story goes on to explain that having a paying job put the idea in her man's mind that he needed a proper last name. Of course, slaves were almost never given a last name, so her man set about figuring out what name he wanted. One day, out of the blue, he informed her, 'Since I'm a free man, I'll be called that, so

I'm George Freeman and 'cause you're my woman, you'll be called Lucy Freeman'."

At this point in the story, Ray always pauses, takes swig of beer, pets the dog if it is near, or begins whittling on a piece of wood and whistling a tune and appearing to have totally forgotten he was telling a story.

"Don't stop now; you're just getting' to the best part." Jo urges.

Ray grins; "You mean when Momma wanted me to take a bath in the washtub?"

Jo nods her head and he picks up the story. "On this particular day, Lucy heard Momma tell me to take a bath in the wash tub as soon as Lucy finished the wash; so when Lucy was done, she called me over. 'Get out of them clothes and jump in the tub; I'll scrub you up good, just like your Momma wants.' This surprised me and made me stammer. 'I can't do that. I'm too old for you to see me naked.' As soon as I said that, Lucy really shocked me by putting her hands on her hips, throwing back her head and laughing real loud. 'Sonny Boy, when I was a slave one of my jobs was to scrub the master's children every Saturday afternoon. Some of them boys was a lot older than you. Get out of them britches and get in here. You ain't got nothin' that I ain't seen a hundred times before'."

At this point in the story Jo always squeals, "Then what, Daddy? Then what?"

Using an exaggerated drawl Ray proclaims; "Why honey chile, what else could I do but shuck my drawers, get in the tub and let her scrub me? But I'm here to tell you, I was very careful never to be anywhere near the tub on washday after that."

Ray, like his father before him, found much satisfaction in tinkering - creating new items and improving existing ones. Ray's kids benefitted from this; he was more apt to express his affection for them by designing and building unique toys and playthings than in bestowing hugs and kisses. The Simmons' kids had toys that were the envy of North Le Grand.

Ray designed a kazoo by folding waxed paper over a comb and showing the kids how to produce music by blowing on it. By using a large four hole button and a length of twine, he created a toy that he called a "zoo-zoo"; by spinning the button around on the twine really fast, the twine jerked, the button gyrated and made a whirring - "zoo-zoo" - sound. By hammering soda bottle caps into the heel and toe of a pair of the kids' shoes, he gave them dancing shoes. Among the other playthings they had were stilts fashioned from 4x4 pieces of wood, tire swings, Tarzan ropes, and sea-saws. Their favorite creation of Ray's was something he caller a "Flying Jenny"; it was a contraption that crossed a sea-saw and an ocean wave - it went up and down at the same time is spun around. In spite of many bruised bottoms and skinned knees, the kids loved it.

CHAPTER 6

Grandma Simmons' Place

Margaret Ann adores her Grandma Simmons; almost every day she unlatches the gate between their yards and goes to visit her, sometimes she stays overnight, even though she has a perfectly good bed next door.

Miz Simmons is small and slender, shaped like Margaret Ann's favorite doll; she wears her long grey hair braided and wrapped into a coronet around her head. Margaret Ann thinks this hairdo was very stylish. She considers her grandmother the prettiest woman in the world, even prettier than the movie stars that she sees when she goes to the movie house with her mother.

One of Margaret Ann's favorite games is one she called "beauty parlor lady"; she plays it many evenings, after Grandma has taken a bath and put on her nightgown and robe. Margaret Ann pretends that Grandma is her customer; she stands in back of the chair where Grandma is sitting, removes all the hairpins, unbraids her hair, brushes it until it is smooth and silky, and pulls it back into a long braid that hangs to Grandma's waist. Margaret Ann thinks that Grandma is as nice as she was pretty; she has a sweet smile, almost never loses her temper, and she never says an unkind word about anyone.

During the 'beauty parlor lady' game, Margaret Ann talks to her Grandma, like she has seen the real beauty parlor lady does when she accompanies her Mother to get a haircut or a wave. One evening she asks, seemingly out of the blue, "Grandma, how come you've got so many names?"

"What ever do you mean, child?"

"I'm named after you; so, one of your names is Ann, but your sisters all call you Annie."

"Well that's only two names."

"Grandma! I'm not done yet."

"Oh, pardon me." Miz Simmons chuckles.

Margaret Ann sighs and admonishes, "Don't laugh at me. Beauty parlor ladies are 'posed to talk to you about stuff like that."

"Sorry, I'll try to be a better customer."

"Good, now where was I? Oh yes, the pastor and some of the folks at church call you Miz Simmons; most everybody else calls you Grandma Simmons; and, cept for me, Jo and Cary, the rest of your for real grandkids call you Mur."

After a brief pause, Grandma Simmons asks, "You done talkin' now Miz Beauty Parlor Lady?"

"Yes, ma'am."

"OK, let me see, my Momma and Daddy named me Ann when I was born; Annie is a nick name for Ann; that's why my sisters call me that. Lots of folks started callin' me Miz Simmons when I married your Grandpa, 'cause he was Mister Simmons. Then, I became a widow woman. Do you know what a widow woman is?"

"Nope."

"It's a lady whose husband is dead."

"OK."

"In these parts, it's considered a sign of respect to call a widow lady 'Grandma'; so I think it's nice that folks want to call me that."

"Me, too."

"Lets' see, where was I?   Oh yes, that's how I got to be Grandma Simons to so many folks. As for Mur, when your cousin Billy Ray was a baby, he couldn't talk real plain and when he tried to say Grandma, it sounded like grammur. Well, we just shortened it to Mur to make it easier for him to say. As the other grandkids came along, they just copied Billy Ray and used that name for me. That's how I got so many names."

"I wonder why I don't call you Mur."

"That's because your mother was raised up real formal and doesn't like usin' nick names; it's just her way."

Miz Simmons is a devout Southern Baptist who attends church services regularly; but, except for all day singin' and dinner on the ground, which she enjoys, she seldom participates in the social activities of the church and has little interest in church gossip when it reaches her ears. She attends church to seek knowledge and to reinforce the integrity of her beliefs, not for social advantage. She believes that religious training is important and she sees to it that Ray's children attend church and Sunday school regularly and that they go to Vacation Bible School each summer.

Her lawn is lush; her flower gardens, with their vast array of colors, are the envy of the neighborhood. Just beyond the lawn and flower gardens, is a small orchard of fruit and nut trees; she planted the orchard in this spot so that the trees would serve as a screen to block the view of the, sometimes messy, chicken yards. Behind the chicken yards, she keeps two hives of bees, and to the left of the chicken yards, she has a vegetable garden.

To Margaret Ann, Jo and Cary their Grandma Simmons's yard is a wonderful playground and they each have favorite things to do there. Margaret Ann likes picking figs, helping Grandma prune the trees, and gathering eggs. Cary's prefers to follow

Grandma around and watch her work in her vegetable garden. Even though he is a very young boy, she talks to him as though he were an adult, pointing out various plants. "Look there, aren't those tomatoes comin' along nicely - won't be long before they are ready to pick. Okra is about ready to pick too, and won't Jo hate that? She says it makes her all itchy to be in the okra patch." Having Grandma talk to him like that, makes Cary feel very grown up. He nods solemnly, as she shares her knowledge about butter beans, beets, bell peppers, red potatoes, turnips, collard greens, and such. Cary loves collard greens, sometimes sneaks into the garden and eats them raw, straight off the stalk.

Sometimes following Grandma around the garden produces a bonus for Cary. Grandma catches a June bug, ties a piece of thread to one of its rear legs and gives it to him to play with. This unique flying "toy" fascinates him and he plays with it for hours before he gives it back to Grandma so she can take the thread off and turn it loose.

Jo, a chatterbox, often shadows Grandma's every move, inside and outside of the house; she never seems to run out of questions to ask or comments to share. She is the only grandchild that Miz Simmons allows out among the beehives; Ray jokes that his mother allows this because, "it's the only time Momma can shut Jo up for a few minutes". Miz Simmons teaches Jo all about bees; important lessons like bees only sting if they are startled or feel threatened. Under her Grandma's tutelage, she learns how to move slowly and quietly among the hives.

Many of the neighborhood kids are afraid of bees and other 'creepy crawly' things, but Grandma Simmons teaches her grandchildren all about these creatures so that they have no fear of them. When she sees Katydids, Grasshoppers, Praying Mantis, Centipedes, June Bugs, or Daddy Longleg spiders, she points them out to the kids and talks about their habits. She shows her grandchildren how to handle them properly so as not to harm them. Another of Grandma's lessons is how to catch Lightenin Bugs; put them in a jar with holes punched in the lid, watch them flicker, then, release them, unharmed, at the end of the evening.

She warns them to never, never, never touch a wasp or poke anything at a wasp nest. Another fun thing that Grandma shows them is how to use spit and a straw to catch Doodlebugs.

CHAPTER 7

The Feed Man

Once a month, a man form the local feed store delivers 25 or 50 pounds of chicken feed to Miz Simmons. Jo, a very observant child, is aware that, on feed delivery day, Grandma always seems to have some chore to do in the house and that she carefully keeps the screen door locked until after the feed man has gone.   She has one of the grandchildren stay on the back porch or in the back yard when the deliveryman arrives; then, she calls, from inside the house, "Just put the feed in the shed for me, please, and if you're hot and thirsty help yourself to water from the pump." To whichever grandchild is nearest the screen door, she says, "Come get this money and pay the man for the feed."

Miz Simmons usually likes to visit a bit with everyone who comes by her house, including the delivery people like the mailman, and the iceman, and old Mr. Hayes who drives the produce wagon. Therefore, Grandma's attitude with the feed man puzzles Jo; so she asks her mother, "Why won't Grandma come outside and talk to that nigger man who delivers her chicken feed? She comes out and talks to everybody else."

Sarah's face turns red, she slaps Jo across the cheek, and sternly demands, "Don't ever let me hear you say that word again, it's not a nice word. You say Negro or you say Colored but don't you dare say nigger again. Do you hear me?"

Jo is too shocked to speak; she just nods her head and runs into the bedroom holding her cheek. The physical sting of the slap didn't upset Jo, the slap wasn't very hard; nor was it the first time Jo had gotten a slap from her Mother. Jo is upset because the slap is so unexpected; she doesn't know what she did to provoke her mother's wrath. When she said Nigger, she was only describing the feed man, who happened to be black.   This mattered not a hill of beans to Jo; she liked the feed man and could have chosen to say 'brown eyed', 'tall', 'skinny', or 'slow moving'; instead, she chose to mimic her Daddy and use a grown up word that she had heard him say.

She sits on the end of the bed rubbing her cheek and sulking for a few minutes while she plans her revenge. Jo is bright child who loves attention and knows how to manipulate situations so that she directs the maximum amount of it her way; she intends to get all the attention she can from this one. She is humming as she goes looking for her beloved Daddy; her plan is to tattle to him, gain his sympathy, and maybe, even get her mother in trouble for slapping her. Her expression changes the minute she sees her Daddy; she puts a sad expression on her face, hangs her head low and whines; "Daddy, Mother slapped me for no reason."

"Now Jo, I'm sure she thought she had a reason; let's see if we can figure out what it is."

"Daddy, there wasn't a reason; she just slapped me and said that I couldn't use the word nigger anymore."

"Well, Honey, I'm not too sure I like her slappin' you but I agree with her about you saying nigger."

"But Daddy, you say it. Why can't I"

"Jo, you can't always do what you want to; nor can you do everything I do.   I say nigger because that's what everybody called colored folks when I was growing up; everybody at the mill calls 'em that; if I suddenly quit sayin' it, folks at work - includin' the niggers will think I'm actin' phony and I see nothing to be gained by that.   My doing or saying something doesn't necessarily make it right for you do it.   So stop acting like a martyr and do as your mother tells you."

CHAPTER 8

Sarah's Folks

Sarah's parents live in the mid-sized South Alabama city of Wilsonville. Larger than Le Grand, Wilsonville, had a wide variety of stores in which to shop, many professional service establishments, a streetcar line, a taxicab company, its own city police and fire departments, and homes with electricity and indoor plumbing.

Sarah's father, Carlton Carrington, is a gentle, hard working man who is liked and respected by his neighbors; he has a twinkle in his eyes, a ready smile, and a round belly that remind his grandkids of Santa Clause. He takes great pleasure in the company of his daughter and grandchildren; and they in turn adored him.

On the other hand, there is Sarah's mother, Margaret Carrington, a tiny tyrant with a perpetual frown on her face; she dislikes her neighbors and picks arguments with them over trivial matters. She rules her home with an iron hand, finds fault with almost everything her daughter does, and shows no affection to her husband or her grandchildren. Gossip fascinates her and she never misses a chance to engage in it. She attends a large Catholic church near her home, almost solely for the social advantage it affords her, and looks down her nose at people of other religions, especially Southern Baptists. She continually expresses concern for the souls of her grandchildren; and, chastises Sarah for allowing Ray's mother to play such an active role in the children's religious training. She makes it very clear that she is pained by the fact that the children aren't being raised in the true church. Yet, when Sarah suggests that her mother help with the cost of transportation and tuition to send the grandchildren to the Catholic school in Wilsonville, Mother suddenly changes the subject.

Sarah's kids love going to Wilsonville; the process of getting ready, walking to the bus stop, and riding the bus is always exciting.

Sarah gets down the galvanized washtub, places it in the middle of the kitchen floor, fills it with nice warm water and scrubs each child until their skin glows pink and their hair squeaks when she runs her hand over it. Next, she helps them dress in their Sunday-go-to-meeting clothes and, sometimes, she curls Margaret Ann and Jo's hair.

When everyone is properly groomed, they begin their trek to the bus stop. This involves walking through the neighborhood; the kids know they look swell - all clean and dressed to the nines. They know too that their playmates, some of whom have never been on a city bus or traveled further than Indian Grove, envy them their trip to Wilsonville.

Across the street from the bus stop is a small grocery store. When the weather is warm, Sarah permits the kids to go over to this store and get a soda pop.

"Here, Margaret Ann, you take the money and y'all go get a cold drink to share. Don't dawdle, the bus will be along soon and ya'll can't take the pop bottle on it, so you have to be done when it gets here."

Asking three kids to share one bottle of pop inevitably leads to arguments and accusations. "Cary is drinking too much every time he gets the bottle" - "Jo won't give the bottle back when it's my turn to drink" - "Did you get spit in the bottle?" - "Wipe the neck of the bottle after you drink, I don't want your cooties."

After a few minutes of this, Sarah intervenes; "Give me that thing", she demands. She takes the bottle, finishes the drink, wipes her mouth on the back of her hand; "There, that ends the fussing, don't it?"

While Sarah is distracted paying the bus driver, Jo heads for the long seat at the very back of the bus. Behind this seat is a big window, by kneeling on the seat and looking out this window, she has a great view.   Inevitably, Sarah realizes that Jo is in the back of the bus and orders, "Nancy Jo, you get back up here, right this second!"

Jo reluctantly leaves the seat with the good view and walks toward the front of the bus.   When she gets within reach, her mother grabs her by the arm and pushes her into the seat next to Margaret Ann.   "You know better than to go into the Colored section of this bus. You can't sit with them."

More often than not, there are no black people on the bus; but if any do board, Sarah glares at them and wrinkles up her nose as they pass her seat; she acts as if they are dirty or smell bad. Jo can see that they are dressed in clean clothes and she never detects any bad aroma coming from them, so she figures that her mother just doesn't like to be around them for some unknown reason.

Carlton Carrington glories in entertaining his grandchildren while Sarah and her mother visit. Most times, he takes them out to front porch, away from his wife's critical eye; here he reads to them, teaches them games - Tiddly Winks, and Fiddle Sticks are their favorites - and gives hard peppermint candy to the kids; he even encourages them to give some of the candy to his cocker spaniels that he affectionately refers to as The Boys.

"Don't let Grandma catch you feeding candy to The Boys, she'll get mad; says they make a big mess with it."

"Why do you call your dogs the Boys? When their real names are Jo-Jo and Junie Boy?" Margaret has always been curious about names; this curiosity included animals, as well as people.

Grandpa thinks a moment; "I'm not really sure; but, I reckon it's the same as your Mother calling you three the Kids."

Jo finds it amusing that one of Grandpa's dogs has a name like hers. "Grandpa, did you name Jo-Jo after me?"

"No", Jo-Jo is older than you are."

Jo wrinkles her nose and giggles, "Well, then did Mother name me after him?"

Grandpa convulses with laughter, "Hardly!   Even if your Mother wanted to do such a thing, your Grandmother wouldn't have allowed it. Your proper middle name is Josephine, Jo is just a nick-name, and your Daddy is the one that gave it to you."

"Why'd he do that?"

"You're sure full of questions today; he named you after, Josephine Baker, a famous singer whose voice he admires. OK?"

 "OK."

Grandpa loves to tell stories; he especially likes to share tales of Sara's childhood with her children. "Did I ever tell you about the time that your mother slipped around behind our back and entered a beauty contest?"

The kids shake their head 'no', and so he continues. "Well, she sure did, when she was just shy of sixteen. She saved money from her baby-sitting job to cover the cost of the entry fee and buy the gown and bathing suit that she would need in the competition. As soon as she saved the needed money, she went downtown, paid her fee, and entered the contest. Then, she arranged with a girlfriend to cover for her, in case your grandma got curious about why Sarah was goin' to town so often."

"Why didn't she just tell Grandma she was in the contest?" Margaret Ann asked.

"Your grandma would never have allowed, what she calls, that type of foolishness. She doesn't approve of beauty contests; she says they are just a way of flaunting yourself. She thinks too much attention makes young girls too big for their britches."

"Did Mother win the contest?"

"Well, sort of, and that's how your Grandma caught on to what she had done."

"What happened?"

"Your Mother didn't win the top prize but she was voted Miss Legs. That means that the judges thought she had the prettiest legs in Wilsonville."

"I bet she was happy about that."

"She was. That is, until the paper came out the next day. There was her picture wearing a bathing suit and showing off her pretty legs. When I saw that picture and realized how hard she had worked to be in that completion, I was very proud. Of course, your Grandma, was fit to be tied; she felt that Sarah had lied, made a spectacle of herself, and disgraced the family"

"What happened? Did Grandma whip her?"

"No, but I had my work cut out for me trying to keep Sarah out of the doghouse. I reminded your grandma that the Mayor and City Council, some of whom are members of our church, sponsored this contest. I told her that Sarah just 'forgot' to tell her about entering the contest and hadn't meant to be disrespectful. Eventually, your grandma calmed down and pretended to the folks at church that the whole thing was her idea."

"So, everything turned out OK?"

"Yep, to this very day your Mother is proud of her nice legs but she's smart enough not to mention it around your Grandma; so no real harm was done."

Grandpa often takes the kids for a leisurely walk around town .while Sarah and her Mother are visiting.   Cary rides in his stroller, with Margaret Ann and Jo walking beside him. Grandpa makes frequent stops to let them rest and to show them off to his cronies who own businesses along Wilson Avenue. Their route seldom varies; they go passed the A&P Supermarket - Albright & Woods Drugs - Woolworth Five & Dime - Tip-Top Dry Cleaners -

Lerner's Dress Shop - The Fair Store - two shoe shops - a furniture store - two beauty shops - a barber shop. After a short visit with the barber and the customers in the barbershop, Grandpa helps them cross Wilson Avenue. On this side of the street, they meander back toward home, passing three movie theaters (two for whites and one for coloreds) - a drive-in hamburger stand - a nice restaurant - a shoe repair shop - the Singer Sewing Center - the Wide Awake Café (a not so nice "juke joint").

When it is hot and muggy, Grandpa doesn't go on Wilson Avenue, instead, he takes them to the municipal park. The park has many shade trees to protect them form the sun and keeps them cool while they play on the swings, slides, and monkey bars. This route takes them by a state liquor store - the public library - city and county office buildings - the offices of doctors, dentists, lawyers, architects, and the city jail.

If Grandpa isn't home when they visit, the kids know that they will have to sit in the front room with Mother and Grandma and they don't like this at all. Sarah is also disappointed if her father isn't home; she worries that the kids will do something to provoke their Grandmother's wrath.

Sarah tells the kids to "sit still and behave while Grandma and I visit". They really, really try to do as their mother asks. They know Grandma gets mad easily and then she fusses at their Mother and they don't like that. Nonetheless, being kids, they find sitting still and not getting fidgety very hard to do.

It is not long before they begin whispering, poking, and giggling; they try to stifle their giggles by placing a hand over their mouth. This draws stern glances from their mother and exasperated sighs from their grandmother. Inevitably, one of them, usually Margaret Ann, will say, "Mother, Jo needs a drink of water"; Jo responds "Uh-uh, it's not me; it's Cary; he is very thirsty." Cary sits there with his hands in his lap looking confused and uncomfortable; he doesn't want any water; he really needs to go pee-pee but is afraid to ask.

Sarah looks annoyed; "You kids just sit there and be nice, you can't be thirsty."

"Oh for Pete's sake, since they've already interrupted our visit, I might as well get them some ice water." Margaret Carrington gets up and heads for the kitchen. "Well, Sarah, are you going to help or just sit there like a bump on a log?"

Margaret Ann is sorry to get her Mother yelled at, but, nobody in North Le Grand has an electric refrigerator and she is fascinated with watching Grandma Carrington as she goes to the refrigerator, takes out a little metal tray, pushes the lever inside of it, and makes tiny cubes of ice pop out. They giggle until Grandma demands, "Stop being silly"; she stands, with her hands on her hips until the kids hang their heads and she feels that they are properly chastised; only then does she finish making ice water and handing a glass to each kid.

Cary sits his glass on the table; he has his thighs pressed together, appears ready to cry as he whispers to his mother, "I've really gotta go pee-pee."

Margaret Ann smiles sweetly and says in a prim voice, "Mother, Dear, I'll go help him, so you won't have to."

Jo glares at her sister, quickly puts her glass of water on the table and pushes Cary out of the room. "No, I'm gonna help him."

"I said it first." Margaret Ann yells, putting her glass on the table and running after her siblings.

Neither sister cares much about helping their little brother with his bathroom needs. Indoor plumbing is a novelty to them, and they will use any excuse to flush the commode and watch the water swirl the pee-pee away

Margaret Carrington complains to her daughter, "Sarah, those children don't care about visiting me; all they want to do is drink water and pee, drink water and pee, drink water and pee, all day long; every time you bring them here. Is there something wrong with them or have you just neglected to teach them how to behave properly?"

CHAPTER 9

The Dragon Picture

One hot August morning, Sarah takes a good look at how much her daughters have grown in the last few months and realizes there is no way that the clothes and shoes that they wore to school last year will fit them any longer. School is starting in less than two weeks and she can't put off a getting the clothes and supplies the girls will need to start the new school term. Whether she likes it or not, a trip to downtown Le Grand is necessary; the stores in North Le Grand and Wilsonville do not stock all the items the girls need. She will have to take the children, because the girls have to try on the clothes to ensure a proper fit.

Sarah inquires, "Miz Simmons, you need anything from Le Grand? I've gotta take the kids shoppin' for school stuff; so it'll be no bother to pick up anything you need."

"Lordy Mercy, I don't envy you; goin' all the way over there in this heat. You're gonna be completely frazzled when you get done." Mis Simmons shakes her head as she eases herself into the rocking chair on the back porch.

"I know, but I reckon it my own fault, I should have done it sooner."

"You getting' any clothes or shoes for Cary this trip?"

"I can't afford to – he'll have to wait 'til later in the year."

"Why don't you let me tend him? You know he is gonna get hot, bored, and cranky before you even get on the bus."

Cary loves staying with Grandma Simmons; he thinks she is the best cook and storyteller in the whole wide world; she, in turn, dotes on her chubby little grandson with pale blonde hair and likes having him around to talk to as she does her morning chores.

Cary spends a busy morning playing with a June bug on a string and following his Grandma as she feed chickens and does other chores; by lunchtime, he is so tired that he almost falls asleep while he is eating. As soon as he finishes the meal, Miz Simmons puts him down for a nap. She decides that it is just too darned hot to do any more chores that day; she makes herself a big glass of lemonade; pulls out a box of old family photographs and takes them out to the back porch to look at while her grandson naps.

Cary wakes and wanders out to the porch rubbing his eyes; Miz Simmons smiles at this rosy-cheeked cherub and, ignoring the heat, she pulls him down beside her for a cuddle. As they cuddle, a picture catches Cary's eye; he points to it and exclaims, "Grandma, you have a picture of ghosts."

"Heavens no child," Miz Simmons picks up the picture and holds it so that he can see it better. "There's no such thing as a ghost. This is a picture of the Le Grande Chapter of the Ku Klux Klan."

She explains that the Klan is a group of brave men who are dedicated to protecting their families and white brethren from uppity niggers. "Now, most niggers aren't bad people." She declares. "It's just that a lot of 'em are weak willed and easily pushed, into becoming uppity and doing bad things."

"Are they wearin' their Halloween Costumes?"

"No honey, that's their robes and hoods they wear; lots of times these men have to get a little rough with the niggers to stop them from actin' uppit and causin' trouble. Some white folks don't hold with treating niggers rough. The Klansmen cover their face and clothes so those folks don't recognize 'em and try stop 'em."

"Miz Velma says that cowards hide their face; are they cowards?"

"Land sake, NO, they're not cowards; I'm surprised that Miz Velma would say such a thing. She was probably talkin' about something else or you didn't hear her right."

Miz Simmons points to a man, in the center of the photo, a man wearing an elaborate robe and hood, and proudly tells Cary, "That man is your Grandpa Simmons; he was the top man, the Grand Dragon, a great leader - certainly no coward. I'm right sorry you'll never get to know him."

Cary keeps staring at the picture; these robed and hooded men fascinate him; but they also scare him and make him feel uneasy. He thinks, 'If Grandpa was a dragon, then I'm sure glad he is not around, 'cause dragons are scary and mean." Cary doesn't say that out loud because, even at his tender age, he senses that saying anything will hurt his Grandma and he loves her way too much to ever hurt her, so he just cuddles closer and shuts his eyes until she puts the picture away.

CHAPTER 10

Ray Leaves Sarah

World War II is raging in Europe; the Indian Grove shipyard is bustling with activity; they are hiring every worker they can get, running three shifts, and still finding it difficult to meet the demand for new ships and parts for existing ones. Like shipyards all over America, the Indian Grove Shipyard is hiring women to fill jobs vacated by able-bodied men and boys who are now serving in the military.

Some of the genteel ladies in Indian Grove deem it scandalous that women are doing "man's work"; it is their opinion that no self-respecting lady would dress in a chambray work shirt and trousers, her hair tucked into a bandana like a common wash-woman, and accompany men over the viaduct to work in a shipyard.

However, these jobs are Godsends for many women struggling to keep their families housed and fed while their husbands and sons are fighting in the war; furthermore, most of these women don't have the time or inclination to care what a group of genteel ladies discuss at their bridge games or club meetings.

Ministers, teachers, and city officials begin praising the women who are supporting the troops by working in the factories and shipyards; newspapers and magazines coin the phrase Rosie the Riveter and revere these women as national heroines. Before long, almost everyone in town is singing the praises of women who "build the boats that keep our boys afloat." The genteel ladies of Indian Grove eventually realize that their neighbors don't share their distain for female shipyard workers; they have to eat crow and they find it a hard dish to swallow.

Indian grove is rapidly growing from a sleepy little town into a busy metropolis. In less than a year, the town has a housing tract, a tavern, a movie theater, and a couple of new stores.

The paper mill is losing good workers, some to military service, others to better paying jobs at the Indian Grove shipyard or other defense related industries, and a few to the booming construction trade. Executives at the mill huddle and devise a strategy for keeping their most valued employees; their strategy includes promotions and salary increases for these employees. In line with this strategy, Ray is promoted, from laborer to Shipping Clerk, and given a nice raise in pay.

Ray's new position requires that he work overtime, sometimes pulling a double shift; he is putting in additional time at his drawing board, and continuing his part-time work as a carpenter. Sarah feels neglected because Ray is spending less and less time with her. When he is home, she nags him about not giving her enough attention; Ray's response to this is to withdraw from her even more.

Sarah often relieves her loneliness by walking into Indian Grove and seeing a movie; sometimes she asked her mother-in-law or Miz Velma to watch the kids; but mostly she takes them with her because she likes to have company on the walk to and from town.

The shortest route to the movie theater takes Sarah and the kids through an affluent neighborhood of large homes with beautifully maintained grounds. If it is dark when they pass through this neighborhood, Margaret Ann will gaze into the windows of the warmly lit houses and try to imagine what life is like for the people who live in them. She and Sarah entertain the younger kids by making up stories about these people.

Margaret Ann points out a pretty house; perhaps the two story, yellow one that has brown trim and big Azalea bushes growing at the edge of the lawn. "Look, over there; see that little boy sittin' by the window in his pajamas? I think he has just finished his bath and is tryin' to talk to his mother into givin' him a bowl of ice cream before he goes to bed. Maybe, they even have a maid who'll get it for him."

"Oh, I think you're right." Sarah joins the fantasy. "They may even have a cook who bakes cookies for the little boy to eat with his ice cream."

"His Daddy might be a big shot over at the shipyard - or he could even own it; he drives a big new car and never works overtime." Margaret Ann's ideal Daddy never has to work overtime or be away from his family at night.

Sarah adds; "I say the woman has fine clothes and goes to the beauty parlor every week."

Margaret Ann takes over. "On Saturdays, the lady and the boy get all dressed up; then, the man drives them all the way downtown; to the Saenger Theater and buys them anything they want from the snack bar before they go in to watch the movie."

Sarah watches how the two younger kids hang on every word of Margaret Ann's tales; she is proud that her oldest child possesses such a wonderful imagination and is so articulate.

Ray and Sarah are spending less time together and when they are together, they usually argue and become angry at each other. After a great deal of soul searching, Ray finally admits that his marriage is not working and there is no way that he and Sarah will ever have a happy or stable life together; so he moves out and sets about ending the marriage.

He gives Sarah the money she needs to maintain her household, even though doing so leaves him with very little money to provide food and shelter for himself. He misses his kids and worries about their welfare. There was no doubt in his mind that Sarah loves the kids, but he is well aware that she lacks the skills, maturity, and emotional stability required to raise them by herself. His mind is somewhat relieved by the fact that Sarah and the kids live between his mother and Miz Velma and they will not allow the kids to come to any real harm.

Miz Velma promises to keep a close watch on the situation at Sarah's house, keep him informed and, if necessary, step in and take over caring for the kids until he can make other arrangements. Ray is most concerned about Cary who is still young enough to require close attention and care. This concern is unnecessary because Cary spends almost every waking moment at Miz Velma's home, which is the safest place for him to be.

As sometimes happens in life, shortly after Ray's divorce and when he least expects it, he finds his soul mate and falls in love. Ray's love is Grace, a tiny woman, standing just a fraction over five feet. Her hair is the color of fine mahogany; her dark eyes glow like soft warm chocolate, when she was happy, but switch to cold jet black when she was angry. Her full name is Grace Angela Jones; she works as a bookkeeper for a large drug firm in Le Grande, a city about twenty miles from Indian Grove and the county seat of Le Grande County. Ray has known Grace's family for years; he and one of her brothers were close to the same age, and, as high school pals they had visited in each other's home. When Ray visited the Jones' home, he paid scant attention to Grace; who was a few years younger than her brother and very shy.

Ray is taking the city bus to Le Grande to his lawyer's, in Le Grande, when he notices Grace sitting in the seat across from him; he says "Hey" and inquires about her family. Before he reaches his stop, he has moved to a vacant seat beside Grace so that they can talk without disturbing other passengers. As they chat, Ray discovers what a lovely and interesting woman she has become; he asks to see her again and she agreed.

Early in their courtship, Ray bestows the nickname Shorty on Grace; and she dubs him Archie. Ray is attracted to Graces physical beauty; however, it is the gentle and affectionate way she treats her family and friends that he finds most endearing. He is thrilled when she extends that same caring affection to him and his children.

Grace, an animal lover, has a special bond with dogs and large jungle cats, and possesses an uncanny ability to communicate with these creatures. She loves to fish and is pleased that Ray, unlike many males, finds nothing strange or "unladylike" in her love of this sport.

As a boy, Ray had often fished with his maternal grandfather but after he got married, he never seemed to have time for it. Being with Grace quickly rekindles his love of the sport and the two of them spend much of their courtship fishing from a riverbank or the beaches along the Gulf of Mexico. As they wait for the fish to bite, they plan their life together; these plans inevitably include Ray's children. Grace shares Ray's belief that he is the more stable parent and that the kids will be better off living with him. She assures him that she will help him create a loving home for them.

CHAPTER 11

The "Ladies" of the Church

The situation in Sarah's home is progressing from bad to worse. She is humiliated that Ray left her; she resents the pity in her neighbors' eyes; and she will not accept the fact that Ray will not change his mind and come home to her. She is overwhelmed by all these emotions and is incapable of making rational decisions about rearing the children. Upon hearing that Ray was seriously dating Grace, she became obsessed with winning him back.

Giving birth to three children has enhanced Sarah's trim figure - softening some angles to attractive curves; she has a knack for applying makeup so that it brings out her natural coloring and shows off her pretty, dark eyes; plus, she likes bright colors and wears them well. When she takes the time to fix herself up, she is a striking woman who turns men's heads without even being aware of it. Her efforts to win Ray back include getting a permanent wave, buying new bright clothes that fit a bit more snugly than her old ones did; wearing make-up at home; and, staying close to Ray while he is visiting the kids.

A group of ladies from the church are not at all pleased with Sarah's new look; nor do they like the way their husbands are eyeing her and offering their help with home repairs and any manly chores that she may need done.

Sarah's efforts to entice Ray back, fail completely and her hope of reconciling with him shattered when he marries Grace a few months later. With Ray married to someone else, Sarah is as lonely as she has ever been in her life.

She begins going out in the evenings with a group of young single women who work at the shipyard. They go to the movie theater and the tavern. Sarah neither drinks nor smokes; nonetheless listening to music and sharing "girl talk" eases her loneliness. She loves to dance, and sometimes she accepts an invitation to dance with one of the male shipyard workers who hang out in the tavern.

"Now, don't take this wrong; y'all know I wouldn't be caught dead in that honky-tonk over in Indian Grove and I don't often repeat gossip", a deacon's wife whispers. She is standing with a group of churchwomen, on the steps of the First Baptist Church. "That young woman who rents a room in the house next door to me said she stepped into that honky-tonk, just long enough to get a glass of water to quench her thirst - before she began that dusty walk home; well, she was shocked by what she saw."

"Oh my, what on earth was goin' on in there?" A member of the group asked.

"I'm not real comfortable talkin' about it; you see, it involved a member of our church."

"Good Gracious, what would possess a Christian man to go into such a place? You reckon he was trying to reach a lost soul?"

"I never said the church member was a man; just so happens, it was a woman."

"It's your Christian duty to tell us if one of our own is seen sinnin' in public so we can put a stop to it before the church gets a bad name."

"Well, I'm not right sure it was sinnin'."

"Oh for Pete's sake, just goin' in a place like that seems like sinnin' to me."

"Well, my neighbor said that Sarah Simmons was sittin' there - all decked out, made-up, and lookin' right at home - laughin' and carryin' on with a bunch of shipyard workers. As she was leavin, my neighbor saw Sarah get up and walk to the dance floor with a man."

"Lordy Mercy! We've got to do something about this. Its gettin' way out of hand and just can't go on. Sarah never was much of a housewife; she's more interested in readin' movie magazines all day or makin' fudge than keepin' house and cookin real meals. I used to see poor Ray goin' off to work with a wrinkled shirt and with no lunch pail - I felt real sorry for him - with such a good Momma and all; then, he picks himself a wife like that."

The church ladies pay a visit to Miz Simmons and tell her all about how scandalous they consider Sarah's behavior. "We hate to be the ones to tell you about all this, but somethin' had to be done. For the sake of your grandchildren, you better have a good talkin' with her and get her to repent her sins."

These ladies know Miz Simmons to be a sweet, kind hearted, Christian woman and they have never seen her fly off the handle before; so they mistakenly believe her to be a shrinkin' violet who will not speak up against injustice. They are in for a big surprise.

"Y'all no more hate to repeat this gossip about Sarah to me than I hate to eat ice cream. Not one of you really wants to help her; you just want to run her down; you're all jealous of the way your husbands look at her. They need a good scoldin' about their lust. What Sarah needs is a little compassion and some Christian understandin' to get her back on track. Unfortunately, not one of you is capable of givin' her that. Get out of my house, stop your mean spirited judgments, and pay attention to your own salvation."

The ladies of the church march out in a huff; they have no intention of following Miz Simmons advice. They have a cause and they are not about to listen to reason; instead, they prevail upon the pastor to expel Sarah from the church.

This act of cruelty is a crush to Sarah. She never speaks to anyone from the Baptist Church again.   Miz Simmons is mortified; but she refuses to desert the church. She holds her head high, escorts her grandchildren to the Church every Sunday, and sees to it that they are included in all the activities and functions it has to offer. Her demeanor dares anyone to try to stop her action or insult her grandchildren. This treatment of their Mother and Grandma scars the Simmons kids much deeper than anyone realizes.

CHAPTER 12

Ray Takes the Kids

Following Sarah's expulsion form the church, Miz Velma worries about Sarah's emotional stability. When she hears that the 'ladies of the church' don't think Sarah has learned her lesson and are once again threatening to contact the juvenile authorities, she alerts Ray immediately.

Ray contacts a lawyer to begin the process of gaining full custody of his kids. He knew that this would not be an easy task; but didn't know that after spending countless hours filling out paper work, attending fifteen court hearings and being declared, "in contempt of court", he would be no closer to getting custody of his children than when he started.

Meanwhile, things are going from bad to worse at Sarah's house and Ray knows that he must remove the kids from there quickly. A family of five will not fit into the small studio apartment where he and Grace are living and he is having no luck locating suitable housing that he and Grace could afford. As a last resort, Ray approaches a mill manager, who was interested in having Ray remodel his summer home and offers to reduce his fee for the project if his family can live on the premises while he does the work. The manager will not be using the house until the work was completed; hence, he is happy to save money by allowing Ray's family to live there.

With housing arranged, Ray contacts his lawyer to explain just how bad things are at Sarah's and plead for help in removing the children. The lawyer stated the obvious. "Well, by now you surely know how hard it is to get a judge to take children away from their mother; factor in your inability to conceal your utter contempt for recent judicial proceedings, and the chances of you being able to legally take custody of your children are, at best, very slim."

"Hell, I'm paying you a fortune. Surely you can come up with some way to help me out?"

"Why don't you just take your children and make Sarah sue you for custody if she wants them back? We have one thing in our favor; we are dealing with a judge who prefers to leave kids in one place until a final custody order is issued; so if you take them, he'll likely let them remain in your care as long as there's any question regarding legal custody. Even if Sarah does sue, you'll retain physical custody while the court proceedings are on going."

"You think that would really work?"

I don't see why not. Sarah's pretty naïve; she will never suspect that you have no legal right to take the children from her. Unless she complains, the court won't know or care that you took your kids under false pretences and you'll have accomplished your purpose by default. If she takes you to court, the judge will find you in contempt of court again and slap another fine on you.

So, I say go for it." Ray went home, talked the idea over with Grace, and they agreed that this was their best option for getting the children out of a bad situation.

CHAPTER 13

Bringin' the Kids Home

Taking the kids proves to be a bit more traumatic than Ray had imagined. He reveals his plan to his mother and asks her co-operation. He wants her to prepare Sarah for the fact that he is coming but not reveal the reason for his visit. Naturally, Miz Simmons wants to support her son; she casually remarks to Sarah, "Ray's stoppin' by to see me when he gets off work this afternoon."

"I reckon he's bringin' that woman to your house with him." Sarah refuses to refer to Ray's new wife by name.

"No, not this time; said he might want to take the kids out somewhere and buy them supper. Maybe you should have them take a bath and change their clothes before he gets here, and it couldn't hurt to do a little laundry and straighten up the house a bit." Miz Simmons hopes her verbal nudge is gentle enough so that Sarah won't take offense and get upset with her.

Sarah, ever the romantic dreamer, hears nothing beyond the fact that Ray's wife isn't coming. In her fertile imagination, she immediately pictures Ray's new marriage in trouble and him coming to her and the kids for comfort. She becomes a whirlwind of activity; barking out orders to the kids.

"Margaret Ann, you clean up those dishes and sweep the floor; you know your Daddy hates a dirty house. Jo, make the beds, dust a little, and maybe pick some flowers to put in that nice vase of ours. Cary, take out that garbage and make sure none of your toys are lying around for your Daddy to step on. I'd better get busy, I've gotta heat some water, get down the washtub, soak in it with my good smelling bath oil; then, I need to find something nice to wear, fix my hair, and get a little lipstick on.

Oh, Lord, it'll be nice to have a man in this house again; I just hate being by myself. You kids can bathe when I'm out of the tub and when your Daddy gets here be sure to tell him how much we need him around here, OK?"

Miz Simmons tried to lower Sarah's expectations and lessen the hurt that she was sure to feel when her fantasy failed to become reality. "Honey, he'll only be over at your house long enough to pick up the kids. Please don't spend a lot of time dolling yourself up; you know he has a wife."

Sarah paid scant attention to her mother-in-law's words. "It's no trouble. I love getting pretty for Ray."

By the time Ray arrived at Sarah's she was a nervous wreck and the kids, responding to her nervous energy, were becoming hyperactive. When Ray explained, well really he fibbed, that the judge wanted him to take the kids 'for awhile, until the church ladies settle down', Sarah's daydream evaporated. She became angry and began berating Ray. "Well, if you hadn't gone off and left me and the kids with no thought of how we were going to survive, we wouldn't be in this mess."

"Now Sarah, you know that that's not so. I've always seen to it that you and the kids have what you need, and we've gone over why I had to leave here, at least a million times."

Sarah became sarcastic. "Oh sure, we have. You try to justify your actions every time I bring up the subject; but, I still don't think you had any right to leave."

"That's water under the bridge, and I'm not goin' into it again. Right now, we need to think of what's best for the kids."

"Your movin' back in here is what's best for the kids. Those church ladies would stop threatin' to take my kids if you lived here with us. Every time one of their husbands offers a little help to me, those women come unglued. They're just jealous of me, you know."

Ray began to pack some of the kids' things, Sarah sat down in a rocking chair and glared at him, and Miz Simmons stood wringing her hands as silent tears ran down her cheeks.

An array of emotions washed over the kids as they bewilderedly looked from one adult to another; they were scared because their mother was angrier than they had ever seen her, sad because their Grandma was so upset, glad to see their Daddy, happy and excited to be going to visit him, and worried about leaving their mother all alone. Ray completed the packing, gave his mother a hug, told the kids to give their mother and their grandmother a hug, and, with the good-byes over, he ushered the kids out the door.

On the Greyhound bus, bound for their new home, the emotions of the day soon caught up with the two younger kids. Jo leaned on her Daddy and fell asleep against his side. Grace, seeing that Cary was loosing his struggle to stay awake, pulled him into her lap, and his eyes closed almost before his mind registered what a comfortable lap it was. Margaret Ann couldn't relax; she kept remembering her mother's anger and worrying about how her mother would manage now that she had nobody around to keep her company. She knew that Daddy had done the right thing, but she was more than a little angry with him for hurting her mother. She kept her eyes straight ahead and wouldn't look at her Daddy.

As the bus pulled into town, Margaret Ann was the only one of the kids to see the sign that read, 'WELCOME TO BAYSIDE. LAND OF 1500 HAPPY PEOPLE AND A FEW GROUCHES'. She muttered under her breath "Right now I'm one of the grouches and I might just stay that way".

As the bus continued through town, Margaret Ann forgot to be mad and became interested in the things she saw out the window; there was a pretty brick elementary school, followed a few blocks later by a small business district that consisted of an auto wrecking yard, drugstore, service station/car repair shop, dry goods store, grocery store and café. At the bus stop just beyond the café, the Simons family got off the bus; with Ray carrying Jo in one arm and the suitcase of their things in the other, Grace carrying Cary, and Margaret Ann trudging along behind them, they made the short walk to their new, borrowed home.

Upon arrival at the house, Ray put the kids to bed; he was sharing a cup of coffee with Grace when he realized that the kids had not had any supper. "Great father I am, the first thing I do is forget to feed the kids any supper."

"Oh stop being so hard on yourself; missin' one meal won't hurt those kids; I bet if any of them were hungry they would have told you. They're physically and emotionally worn out right now and the thing they need most is sleep."

"You think so?"

"Yes, I think so; now if you forget to give them any breakfast in the mornin' that's a different matter; I just may have be like the 'ladies of the church' and turn you in to the authorities."

"Funny lady; you know that you don't want me in more hot water with that ole judge that keeps tellin' me I'm in contempt. He just might lock me up; then, who would help you raise those kids sleepin' in there?"

"I reckon you're right. Let's get to bed so we will be ready to make a proper breakfast for them in the mornin'."

CHAPTER 14

What to Call Grace

On their first morning as a family, Grace makes breakfast while Ray sits at the kitchen table talking with the kids. "Yesterday was no fun for any of us: I'm real sorry about that; but, I couldn't figure any other way to stop what those 'ladies of the church' had put into motion with their holier than thou, meddlesome ways. I couldn't leave you kids in the middle of that meanness; so I brought you here 'cause those ole biddies don't want to mess with me."

Grace interrupts him, "Archie, your Momma still goes to that church; sometimes less is better than more – stick to the facts, OK?"

"It's Ok Daddy. We don't like those ladies much either". Jo assures her Daddy.

Margaret Ann is still worrying about her mother. "When exactly are you gonna take us home, Daddy?"

"I'm not takin' you back to your mother's; this is your home now."

Margaret Ann looked shocked. "Mother won't let you do that; we have never lived anywhere without her."

"I know that your mother loves you and isn't gonna like havin' y'all gone, but I just can't let you live with her anymore. I'm gonna' talk real plain now and hope it helps ya'll understand what is going on."

Ray patted Margaret Ann's arm, looked directly at her, and spoke very gently. "You know that your mother hasn't been takin' proper care of you. She simply doesn't know how to raise kids without a lot of help. Your Grandma and Miz Velma tried to warn her that the 'ladies of the church' were really upset… and… well, that didn't work.   She got mad and refused to pay any attention to their offers to help her. I can't put up with that sort of thing; I've gotta know that y'all are gettin' the kind of care you need.   Livin' with me seems like the only way that I can be sure that happens; so, ya'll will stay with Grace and me from now on."

"But Daddy, Mother won't be happy without us."   Margaret Ann protested.

"Maybe for a little while she won't, but she'll soon adjust, Honey.   She's gonna be movin' back into town – either Indian Grove or Wilsonville – and gettin' herself a job.   When she gets busy workin' and seein' more of her folks and her old friends, she'll be OK."

"What's gonna happen to the rest of our stuff?"

"I'll make a trip out there and get it all before she moves out."

"I have to go with you and make sure you get everything."

"Not this trip, Honey, I can manage, and if I do forget anything; Momma will keep it for us 'til the next time we go see her."

"How come you can visit Grandma but we can't see our mother?"

Ray became slightly exasperated; sighed wearily and gave Margaret a curt response.

"Margaret Ann, nobody said you couldn't see your mother. Once she gets settled into her new place, I expect she'll want to have you kids visit her and I'll certainly go along with it. You kids will see her and your Carrington grandparents often. So stop frettin' and concentrate on settlin' in here for now, OK?"

Margaret Ann wasn't really happy: she felt that her Daddy should let her go with him when he went to get their stuff, and she sure didn't like having to wait awhile before seeing her mother, but she didn't want to keep arguing with her Daddy , so she mumbled a reluctant, "Alright."

Ray brought up another subject that he felt needed to be discussed. "I'm sure that ya'll have heard bad things about step-mothers and are wonderin' if Grace is gonna be like that. It's important that you understand that those are just 'make up' stories, kinda like fairy tales. You kids have nothin' to fear from

Grace; she loves you, and she hopes that in time ya'll can learn to love her, too. She has always known that I'm a package deal and that you kids are the rest of the package. She's glad that I brought ya'll to live here, and she wants to help me raise ya'll to be strong, healthy and happy people."

Grace entered the conversation at this point, "Ya'll don't really know me yet and probably don't like me very much right now, but that's OK; I can't say that I blame you. I'm not gonna ever try to take your mother's place. I just want ya'll to give me a chance and see if you can't find a special place for me in your life; 'cause I plan to be around a very long time. Now, you kids can't keep on callin' me 'Mrs. Simmons' or referring to me as 'Daddy's wife'. So let's decide what to call me."

Margaret Ann quickly informed her; "I sure don't think we ought to call you Mother."

The remark startled Grace and she exclaimed, "Oh! I wasn't expecting you to call me that."

Ray realized that Margaret Ann felt duty bound to protect her mother's rights, and he quickly interjected; "Why don't you kids just call her Grace? She'll be the only grown up that you're allowed to address by the first name; that'll make it special without takin' anythin' away from your mother."

"One last thing that ya'll need to know right up front is; this house is just temporary. We'll only be living here while I do some remodeling work; then, we have to move."

"Will we be movin' far away, Daddy?" Jo wanted to know.

"We're already far away, aren't we?" Cary inquired.

This caused everybody to laugh and helped relieve the tension. Chuckling over his son's rather astute observation, Ray responded; "We'll be closer to lots of the family when we move. We're gonna' live in Tannerville, right behind your Aunt Lilly Ann, in that house that your cousin, Billy Ray, and I are buildin'."

Ray reached over and ruffled Margaret Ann's hair. "It's much closer to your mother than you are right now. That'll suit you a little better won't it?"

"Yep." Margaret Ann smiled back at her Daddy, much happier now that she knew what to expect. Jo and Cary really didn't much care about the future; they just wanted to get all this talk over with so they could go explore their new surroundings.

CHAPTER 15

Why Can't I Ride?

The Simmons found Bayside to be a pleasant place to live. East of the small business district, was an agricultural area named Golden Valley; populated mostly by large farms and orchards that produced pecans, walnuts, potatoes, tomatoes, corn, and a large variety of melons. The shores of Le Grande Bay, on the west end of town, were lined with the homes of doctors, lawyers, business executives, skilled tradesmen, school teachers, local politicians and those wealthy enough to have a summer place at the shore. Near a lovely spot of shoreline, where several fresh water streams flowed from the low bluffs that rimed the beach, was a municipal park and wharf. The streams were rich in iron and gave the area a unique tangy, rust-like aroma that was not at all unpleasant.

The Simmons's house was just above the shore on a low bluff. Part of Ray's remodeling project was to build a wharf on the private beach in front of the house. This job was virtually impossible for one man working alone to accomplish; so, Ray set about hiring a nigger from the paper mill to help him. He approached a fellow named Daryl, who was poorly educated but intelligent, hard working and possessed an easygoing manner that Ray liked.

"Want to earn a little extra money?"

"Anytime I can, but what do I haf to do?"

"I need some help buildin' a wharf over at Henry's house. It's mostly just haulin' lumber and swingin' a hammer."

"'Bout how long will ya'll need me for?"

"I reckon three or four week-ends will do it"

"Ya'll got yoself a helper, Mister Ray."

Since it was summer and there was no school, Jo and Cary, age nine and six respectively, alternated their time between playing with friends at the municipal wharf and hanging around the beach in front of their house watching their Daddy and Daryl work. Margaret Ann, at twelve, considered herself too grown up to hang out with her younger siblings all the time; so after an hour or two on the beach with them, she would spend the rest of the day sitting on the large shady porch reading, sewing or writing letters to her mother and friends from North Le Grande.

Jo was very taken with Daryl. Her previous exposure to blacks was limited to Grandma Simmons's feed man, an elderly man who sometimes came to the neighborhood looking for yard work, and the ones she encountered on the bus when going to visit Grandma and Grandpa Carrington. Daryl was very different from any of these black folks; he was a strikingly handsome man in his late twenties. He had very black skin; the body of an Olympian, and whitest teeth that Jo had ever seen. As he worked, his muscles rippled and the sun played over his skin, reflecting a blue undertone when it struck at a certain angle. He had a wonderful smile that displayed his beautiful white teeth, and was always friendly to Jo and Cary in a quiet, respectful way.

Ray and Daryl anchored the pilings in the mud, attached support beams to them, and then they were ready to begin putting in place the planks that made up the surface of the wharf. They began this job at the bay end of the wharf and worked back to the beach. The easiest way to get the planks to the end of the wharf was to place them in the water, a few at a time, and guide them as they floated out.

Daryl noticed that Cary was closely watching how he floated the planks. "Want a ride on my shoulders while I float these planks out? That way you can see more of what I'm doin'."

"Oh Yeah!" Cary answered gleefully.

"OK, hop on."   Daryl bent down low so that Cary could climb up onto his shoulders.

"Wow, I can see way across the bay from up here", squealed Cary as Daryl stood up and began to wade out, pushing the planks ahead of him as he went.

When he got to the end of the wharf, Daryl reached up, took Cary from his shoulders and stood him on the wharf. Cary watched closely as Daryl lifted the planks into place and began nailing them. When he was finished, Daryl lifted Cary back onto his shoulders and gave him a ride back to the beach.

Jo, who had been watching this activity from the beach, felt that Cary was getting too much attention from her hero, Daryl.

"Next trip, I get to ride on your shoulders." Jo informed Daryl in her best miss prissy voice.

"Unh-unh, I can't be touchin' no little white girl; much less lettin' her ride on my back."

"Why not?"

"Ain't proper for no nigger to touch no white girl. It makes white folks mad."

"I don't give a fig who gets mad; I wanna ride like Cary did." Jo stamped her foot for emphasis.

"No child, you can't ride and that's all they is to it. It ain't safe."

"Silly, of course it's safe. You're strong and won't drop me. Even if you did, I can swim."

"It's me that it ain't safe for, not you."

"That's just plain crazy."

Ray had been listening to this exchange and decided it was time to put an end to it. "Whoa there Jo, you don't need to understand, you have to do what Daryl says."

"But Daddy, I don't see no harm in me ridin' like Cary did."

"Honey, listen to me good and mind what I'm about to tell you; don't ever argue with Daryl or any nigger when they say no to you. They know better than you or I what can happen when some white folks think they get uppity or behave improperly."

"Well, I sure don't like it."

"Neither do I but its how things are and for now we have to just live with it, OK?"

Jo's reluctant "OK" was uttered in a disgusted tone and she flounced off in a huff to find Grace and see if she wanted some company.

CHAPTER 16

Livin' In Bayside

The Simmons's spent many afternoons on the newly built wharf; bonding as a family. Grace told the kids how much fun fishin' was and showed them some of the finer points of the sport; like how to bait a hook, how to cast a line and the art of properly using the reel to land a fish once it was hooked. She also enjoyed sitting quietly and listening to Ray talk to the kids.

"OK, here's my rules about fishin'. If you don't bait your own hook - you don't fish, never cast your line close to where someone else is fishin', and you clean what you catch."

"You mean you won't clean 'em for us?" Jo shrunk back in horror.

That's right; everybody who shares the fun of catchin' fish has to share in the chore of cleanin' 'em. I'll help each of you clean the first few so you can learn how it's done; then you're on your own."

"Yuk", Jo walked over to where Grace was sitting; plopped down beside her, rolled her eyes and wrinkled up her nose in a private 'Daddy's crazy' gesture. Grace put her hand over her mouth to smother a giggle. She was happy that Jo had chosen to share this little secret with her and gave her a quick hug.

Ray had no use for crab pots; claiming there was no sport in catching crabs that way. Instead, taught his kids to catch crabs the way his grandfather had taught him. "Use soup bones as bait, carefully tie a bone to the end of a piece of strong twine, lower it into the water, and wrap the other end of the twine around one of these nails that I've put into the side of the wharf. Then you lay on your belly and have your net in easy reach. You have to be really still for about fifteen minutes - or if the water's clear enough - until you see a crab take the bait; then, gently slide your hand under the string, and very, very slowly begin raising it to the top of the water"

He showed them the hand-over-hand movement that would slide the bait smoothly through the water. "Look down at the bait as you do this and if the crabs are feeding; you will be able to see them hanging on the soup bone. When you learn to play the bait right, the crab won't realize that it's moving; he'll be too busy eating. Crabs are greedy creatures and, unless they sense danger, they'll just hold on and keep eatin' as the bait comes up."

"Why do we have to lay on our belly?" One of the kids wanted to know.

"Two reasons; first if you stand up, you make a shadow on the water and the shadow will spook the crab; and he'll let go of the bait and return to the bottom of the bay. Second, if you want to land the crab you're gonna have to be close enough to the water to work a net under him before he sees you doing it."

The kids spent hours practicing crabbin'; at first, they lost more than they landed but, with time, their skill improved and they got so that they landed almost every one that took the bait.

Playing around the yard one afternoon, Cary happened upon a small snake – about six inches long and about as big around as a pencil. He had seen only one or two snakes in his young life and was very curious about this one. He gently picked it up, the way his Grandma had taught him to do with 'critters' and took it onto the screen porch to examine it and play with it for a while. He let the snake slither freely about on the porch but when it went in a direction not to his liking – like toward the screen door, as though to return to the ground – he would talk gently to it and nudge it back toward the center of the porch; "It's Ok little guy. I won't hurt you and I'm gonna let you go back outside soon. I just want to get to know you better."

While Cary was engrossed with the snake, Grace came out onto the porch; she looked closely at the snake that Cary was playing with and began slowly backing away. As she backed away, she called out quietly but urgently, "Ray, come out on the porch right now and come out real slow and easy."

Ray, hearing the worried undertone in Grace's voice, did as she requested. He walked slowly out to the porch, stood beside Grace and became very alarmed. White faced, his voice slightly trembling, he softly addressed his son, "Cary, please leave the snake where it is and come over here with Grace and me for a minute."

"I can bring him to you", Cary offered. "He's not afraid of me and he don't bite or nothin' like that."

"No son, just leave the snake where it is and walk slowly and steadily over to us. Don't make any sudden moves or try to pick up the snake."

Sensing that there was a problem, Cary did exactly as he was told and when he was safely away from the snake, Ray walked slowly over to it and, though he knew he was taking a chance on being bitten; he gently picked it up, cupped it in his hands, walked outside and placed it on the ground.

Ray, white faced and visibly shaken, came back onto the porch. "Son, the snake that you were playin' with was a baby water moccasin."

"Well, he sure was cute. I hope I can find him again."

"Cary, you have to stay away from water moccasins; they're highly poisonous snakes. You and I are both very lucky that it didn't bite us. I kinda thought that your Grandma Simmons had taught you about snakes but guess I was wrong."

"We never saw any snakes around her house."

"Well, come on inside so we can get out my book on snakes and go over it together. You need to know which ones to steer clear of in the future."

That was the beginning of Cary's education on snakes. Ray taught him that he needn't be afraid of snakes but he must be able to identify and avoid direct contact with the dangerous ones. He admonished Cary not to provoke snakes and to try to give them the space to go on their way without upsetting them. "Snakes have as much right to live in this world as we do, they usually avoid people and won't be aggressive to a person unless they are startled or provoked."

CHAPTER 17

Jubilee

As fall approached, the Simons kids began to hear folks in the neighborhood talk about 'Jubilee'; from the snatches of conversation that they overheard, it seemed that Jubilee was a big deal in the town. The subject of Jubilee came up one afternoon when Margaret Ann, Jo and Cary were sitting on the beach with a bunch of their new friends.

"What's this Jubilee thing that's got everybody all excited?" Margaret Ann asked.

A kid who had always lived in Bayside, looked at her in surprise; "You never heard of Jubilee?"

It sounded to Jo like this kid was implying that her sister was dumb or something so she said, "If she had, do you think she would've asked about it, dummy? We don't have anythin' called that where we come from, so how are we supposed to know about it?'

Another kid in the bunch remarked, "Aw, don't get all huffy, he didn't mean no harm; he's just surprised is all."

"Fine", retorted Margaret Ann, "but we still don't know what the heck Jubilee is so maybe y'all can just answer the question."

"Sure, it's when flounders, eels, and bay crabs all jump out of the bay and into buckets that we hold in the shallows."

All three of the Simons kids began laughing and Cary said, "Boy y'all must really think we are dumb if you think we believe that."

Well, it's so, just ask anybody in town; they'll tell you."

"I'm gonna ask my Daddy as soon as I get home and I bet he's gonna say that y'all are full of it and just tryin' to fool us."

As soon as they got home, Jo walked up to Ray; "Daddy, a bunch of kids down at the beach told us that sometimes fish just jump out of the water and right up into buckets that folks around here hold in the shallow water. Have you ever heard such a thing?"

"Actually I have, it's called Jubilee. I've known about it for most of my life; I reckon I just took it for granted that somebody had told y'all about it. Just last week, I ran across something about it in a book I was reading; go in the house and get the book by my chair, and y'all can read up on it.

"Are you pullin' my leg?"

"No, Jo, I'm not, go on in and get the book and you'll see."

Jo got the book; she, Margaret Ann, and Cary went out on the screened porch and Margaret Ann read it aloud to them.

The book said that Bayside is one of two places in the entire world that experiences the rare phenomenon, called Jubilee. A Jubilee occurs when certain species of marine life, literally, jump or scurry from the water. The Bayside Jubilee is reputedly caused when run off from heavy autumn rains in the upper part of the state cause the four large rivers, which empty into the mouth of

Le Grande Bay, to dump an abundance of metal & mineral rich water into the bay.

Once in the bay, this mineral rich fresh water mixes with salty Gulf water and, when temperature and atmospheric conditions are just right, a mild electrolytic charge is set up in these waters. This charge irritates the very sensitive gills of flounders, eels, and bay crabs, causing them to jump or scurry from the water to get away from it. The flounders and eels jump from the water and pile up at the mouths of the streams that flow into the bay, and the crabs simply scurry out onto the beach to wait out the irritation. The temperature/atmospheric conditions necessary for a Jubilee occur only on early autumn mornings, just before dawn; at dawn, the electrolysis is broken up by the sunlight striking the water and the Jubilee is over. When a Jubilee happens, seafood lovers simply stand in shallows of the bay, and hold tubs or buckets so that the fish land in them as they jump from the bay water.

When Margaret Ann finished reading, the Simmons kids were silent for a minute, and then Cary exclaimed, "Wow, no wonder

Jubilee is such a big deal to folks in town; I can hardly wait to see it."

To ensure that town folks don't miss this annual chance to gather large amounts of seafood for practically no effort, residents of Bayside and nearby towns set up a 'Jubilee watch', during the early autumn months.   On the beach, just beyond Bayside Municipal Park, city workers build large campfires; provide hot dogs, chips and soda to local kids, teens and young adults who will sit around the campfire all night. This group rotates watch duty so that someone is always awake to observe the first signs of marine life attempting to escape the bay. As soon as this begins to happen, the group on the beach runs up the bluffs and into town banging metal pot lids together, whistling and shouting "Jubilee!" When the town folks hear these shouts, they grab their washtubs and buckets and rush down to the bay to catch flounder and eel as they jump from the water and gather up the crabs as they scurry up onto beach.

The remodel job that Ray was doing was completed in late summer. By early autumn, the family was preparing to move out of their borrowed home. A group of neighborhood kids invited Cary to an overnight camp-out on the beach. It was just a few boys from the neighborhood and their "camp" was within sight of the house of one of the boys, so Grace and Ray saw no harm in allowing Cary to attend. While these impish boys sat, huddled close around their campfire to ward off the evening chill, Cary mentioned how sad he was to be moving before Jubilee time.

"That's a bummer. Jubilee is the most fun thing around here."

"Yeah, ain't you never seen one?"

"Never even heard of one 'til we moved here."

"Do you reckon your folks would let you stay with one of us so you can see it?"

"Naw, they won't let me come back; it'll be too far from our new house."

"Hey, I've gotta idea."

"What?"

"Nope, probably it won't work; y'all would be too chicken?"

"Whose chicken?"

"We could play like there's one right now?"

"Are you nuts? We will get skinned alive if we do somethin' like that."

"I knew y'all was chicken."

"I ain't no chicken; I dare the rest of y'all to do it."

"What if we get caught?'

"We all blame it on the other one; that way they won't know who to be mad at?"

"He's right and I double dog dare y'all."

After a bit more "darin' and double dog darin', the boys agreed that it sure would be fun and it would give Cary a send off that he wouldn't forget.

So they raced up the bluff and through the residential district shouting "Jubilee!"

It was rare, but not unheard of, for Jubilee to occur this early in the fall; therefore, when these boys ran up the bluff, about 4am, shouting "Jubilee", many folks rushed to the beach only to discover that they'd been hoodwinked.

A few town folks complained to Ray about the behavior of Cary and his friends. Ray promised to 'speak sternly to the boys about this'. However, even as he was listening to the complaints, Ray had a hard time holding back a grin; this was so like some of the pranks he and his buddies had pulled when they were young. He knew the boys weren't being malicious, just letting off some steam and acting in the spirit of harmless fun.

CHAPTER 18

Gettin' to Know Tannerville

Ray's family moved into the house next-door to his sister, Lilly Ann, and her family in Tannerville. His brother, Wilton, lived just down the block with his wife, Bessie.

Tannerville was an oddly configured town that appeared to have grown in a haphazard manner rather than by any design or plan. There was an affluent white neighborhood at the south end of town; doctors, lawyers and high-level mill managers lived in this area.   To the north, separated from the affluent neighborhood by three churches and a small business area, was the working class white neighborhood where Ray and his siblings lived. This working class neighborhood was wedged in between two black sections; the black section on the west end of town was called the Quarters and the one to the east was called Paper Mill Village. Just beyond Paper Mill Village was the paper mill where Ray, and more than half of the residents of Tannerville, worked.

The day after Ray's family moved in, Lilly Ann's two youngest sons, Wayne Junior and Jerry, came over to check things out and spend some time with their cousins.

"Uncle Ray, can yore kids go explorin' with us?' Wayne asked.

"What do you mean by explorin'?" Ray wanted to know.

"Aw, you know, just showin' them around our part of town and helpin' them find out where everything is."

"Sounds like a fine idea to me, but check with Shorty, OK?"

Wayne looked puzzled; "whose Shorty?" he wanted to know.

"That's what he calls Grace." Cary informed his cousin.

"Why?"

"I don't know – grown-ups just do silly stuff, sometimes."

"Yep."

"Come on; let's go see if she'll let us do it."

Grace granted permission and the kids all took off, with Wayne and Jerry in the lead.   First, they went to a large grassy meadow with a small stream running trough one end of it. This meadow spanned the working class white residential section and the Quarters; therefore, all the town kids, black and white, played in it.

"This here's The Field and everybody plays in it. You're gonna see lots of nigger kids here, but don't worry about 'em; they mostly leave us alone and play down in their end of The Field, by Quarters and we play up here in ours."

"Does it have a name?" Cary wanted to know.

"Huh?"

"You know like in Bayside, our park was named Bayside Municipal Park."

"Naw, this ain't no park, it ain't even a real playground. There's a playground over behind the school and there's a little park across from Longs Grocery; we'll show y'all later. This here is just an old empty field; reckon its named The Field. At least, that's what everybody calls it."

"Don't y'all ever play with the Negro kids?" Jo asked; since the day her Daddy had upheld her Mother's order not to say nigger, she was careful about using it.

"Well, sometimes when there's no grown ups or prissy, 'tattletale' kind of white kids are around we all play dodge ball, baseball or tag together."

When they completed their tour of The Field, the kids walked over to the elementary school, they passed a couple of produce stands, an ice cream parlor, a gas station, small grocery store and a honky-tonk.

This is where y'all will go to school 'til you get out of seventh grade, then you go over to Viking High in Wilsonville." Jerry told his cousins.

"Looks like a pretty nice school." Margaret Ann offered.

"Yeah, we like it OK." Wayne told her. "If you go all the way around behind the school's baseball field, you end up in the little park over by Longs Grocery. We'll go that way another time; Momma gave me money to buy y'all a fountain Coke at the drug store; so we're gonna go over there next."

So the five cousins, crossed the street, walked passed another gas station and went into the drug store.

"Wow, this lunch counter is better than the one at Sermon's Drug in Bayside." Jo was impressed with the long polished counter that was so tall that the kids had to climb up on high stools to sit at it."

When they were done drinking their fountain Cokes and looking over the merchandize in the drug store, they checked out more of the town, a dry cleaners, JB's barber shop, a beauty shop and Longs Grocery - the BIG store in town.

"We like Longs; the lady that runs it is real nice when we go in there to shop with Momma.   If we're up this way without Momma, and we go in and get a drink of water from the fountain in back; she don't mind or nothin' and sometimes she even gives us free candy. Her husband is a deacon at the church where we go and we like him pretty good too." Jerry informed his cousins.

Walking passed the drug store on their way back to Ray's house, Wayne pointed across the street. "Oh, I almost forgot; see that bench over there? That's where the bus that goes to downtown Le Grande stops."

The Simmons kids later learned that this bus stop was another area of Tannerville where black and white kids sometimes mingled. At the bus stop they would joke around with each other or play quick game of 'Simon Sez' as they waited for the bus. If a grown up arrived at the bus stop, this action ceased immediately and the kids separated into two groups, based on color. When the bus arrived, the white kids got on first and took seats near the front and the black kids instinctively moved to the seats in the back of the bus. This seemed to happen automatically and neither group of kids ever thought to question why, it was just how things were done and they accepted it.

From Tannerville it was an easy walk to Wilsonville, where Sarah now lived, and within a week of moving to Tannerville,

Ray took the kids over to Wilsonville so they could see where their mother lived and worked.

After giving the kids money for hamburgers and cokes, Ray left them in front of the Main Street Café, where Sarah worked as a waitress. The kids had lunch and a nice visit with their mother while Ray ran a couple of errands and did a little shopping.

While Ray and the kids walked home to Tannerville, he chatted with them about visiting Sarah.

"I bet your mother was happy to see y'all; did you enjoy your visit?"

The younger two nodded their heads and Margaret Ann answered, "Yes, Daddy. It was fine,"

"I expect that ya'll will be coming over to Wilsonville often – to go to the movies, use the swimming pool and such. It's OK with me if you stop by and visit your mother when you're over this way but ya'll have to understand that she has a job, an apartment to take care of, and her own social life now. She won't be able to visit every time you're over here; especially when she's workin' at the café, so if she says that she's busy, just say a quick 'Hi' and don't hang around making pests of yourselves."

Grace looked at life differently than most of her neighbors; none-the-less, she enjoyed life in Tannerville. Her neighbors considered fishin' to be a man's sport; not Grace, she never passed up a chance to fish. Anytime that Ray suggested they go fishin', she could round up the kids, pack a picnic lunch, check her fishin' gear and beat him to the car. She felt no guilt about letting the kids skip Sunday school so the family could spend the day fishin' at Gulf Shores, whenever Ray was lucky enough to have a Sunday off from the mill.

Grace was an excellent homemaker; but she did it her way, and didn't worry that her neighbors did things differently. She did her gardening and other outdoor chores in the morning or early afternoon and did the ironing and most of her housework late at night, after the kids were in bed.

Delta blues was Grace's music of choice and she listened to it on the radio while she cooked dinner and did her evening chores. Her neighbors called Delta blues nigger music and publicly shunned it. However, many of them secretly enjoyed listening to the blues coming from her radio, and if anyone looked closely, more than a few of Grace's neighbors could be observed humming under their breath and swaying to the beat as they prepared dinner or sat out on their porch to catch an evening breeze.

Jo had never heard any delta blues before she met Grace, but she soon learned to love that throbbing, heart tugging music as much as Grace did.

CHAPTER 19

Grace Bonds with the Kids

Grace's mother died when Grace was a very young girl. Her father coped with the loss of his wife by drinking heavily; this put Grace in the position of having to raise her younger siblings, almost single-handedly, and in so doing, she developed a knack for getting children to do chores without having to nag or fight with them about it.

Shortly after moving to Tannerville, Ray had a dump truck load of good loam delivered and dumped in a corner of the yard.

Grace intended to use part of this dirt for her flower garden and use the rest to build up a low spot in the lawn.

Grace took one look at this huge mound of dirt, and began planning how she would get the kids to help her with the distribution of this dirt.

She remembered how well making work into a game and tossing in a little bribery worked with her siblings, so she used this approach with her step-children. "I'll treat you kids to Cherry Kool Aid and donuts if you help me move some of that dirt. Y'all can shovel it into the wheelbarrow; take off your shoes and kick it around; jump on top of the pile and slide down it; you can even throw it at each other as long as you don't throw any higher than the shoulders."

"You don't care how dirty we get?" Cary wanted to know.

"Nope, I'll even hose y'all down when you're done."

"Can Wayne and Jerry play on the dirt pile with us?"

"Yep, if your Aunt Lilly Ann don't care."

"What about other kids in the neighborhood?" Jo wanted to know.

"They're all welcome, as long as their parents don't mind. I'll even give them Kool Aid and Donuts."

"Are you gonna' give 'em the ones you got for us or get some more?" Jo had a real sweet tooth and didn't relish sharing part of her treat with anyone.

 "I'll walk up to Longs Grocery and get some more donuts and make an extra pitcher of Kool Aid; don't worry Jo there'll be plenty for all of y'all."

Within an hour, the yard was full of yelling kids, half the dirt pile was spread around, and the kids didn't even realize that they had been doing yard work. Ray walked out of his shop, looked around in amazement, and asked Grace. "How did you get the kids to do all that?"

"All I did was bribe them with Kool Aid and donuts, tell them I didn't care how dirty they got; then, I just got out of the way and let 'em do it any way they wanted."

"Well it sure worked; they're all havin' fun. Let's go bring out the Kool Aid and donuts."

As the kids sat in the back yard eating the donuts, Ray sat down by Elvin, one of the boys who lived next door and dryly advised; "Elvin, be sure you don't eat the hole."

Elvin nodding his head, solemnly replied, "OK, Mister Simmons." He then began carefully nibbling at the outer edge of his donut, being careful to leave a narrow strip of it around the hole.

Elvin's older brother gave Ray a puzzled look, stared at his brother in disbelief; and finally began to laugh and shout, "Don't eat the hole; don't eat the hole; you got ole Elvin with that one; it's a good joke; don't eat the hole. I'm gonna' try it on some of my friends next time we eat donuts."

CHAPTER 20

The Blues

When white kids who lived in Tannerville went to Wilsonville, it was acceptable for them to walk through the Quarters because it was, by far, the shortest and most direct route. However, when a late afternoon movie or an evening football game kept any of them in Wilsonville after dark, most white parents would arrange to pick them up or instruct them to "stay in a group and go around the long way. I don't want ya'll in the Quarters at night". Ray, however, told his kids; "You're perfectly safe in the Quarters at night. There's not a nigger over there would harm a white child.   Besides, they mostly all know me from the mill and they recognize you as my kids, so they'll keep an especially close eye on ya'll and help you out if you ever need it. Ya'll just come on home the same way, day or night."

Along the route from the Simmons house to Wilsonville, was a juke joint, called the Blue Moon Café; anytime Jo heard the sound of blues music issuing from the jukebox in this café, she would walk real slow and enjoy the music. One hot July afternoon as Jo approached the café, she heard piano music that she was pretty sure wasn't coming from the jukebox; she eased around until she could peep in the open door, and sure enough, the music wasn't coming from a jukebox. A black man, so huge that his ample backside took up the entire piano bench, sat playing the old piano in the corner of the café. It was just an old Baldwin piano, probably out of tune, but to Jo it sounded awesome. She couldn't resist stopping and listening; never had Delta Blues sounded so mournful. Her eyes got all teary and her heart ached as the piano player did a medley of Ruth Brown songs – "Daddy – Daddy", "Oh What a Dream" – "Mama He Treats Your Daughter Mean". Jo's sadness lifted when he shifted from blues to 'boogie-woogie'. His fingers flew and that old Baldwin rocked as he hit a Big Joe Turner lick with "Flip, Flop, and Fly". By the time he got to "Pine Top Boogie" and "Boogie-Woogie Stomp" everybody in the place was dancing.

The waitress noticed Jo standing in front of the café listening to the music; she walked out with an RC Cola in her hand.

"Are you gonna run me off? I don't mean no harm. I just love your music; some of it makes me sad, but, lots of it makes me want to snap my fingers and shuffle my feet." Jo smiled shyly at the waitress.

"Bless yore heart honey, you sure talk real honest and I know what you mean. Them ole blues and boogie-woogie tunes can sure get yore heart pumpin' and yore feet moving. White folks mostly don't pay no attention to the blues or the boogie woogie, and they don't understand how good it is for the soul; but you do, don't you sugar pie?"

"Yes ma'am, I reckon I do, 'cause I sure love listenin' to it."

"Don't be callin' me ma'am. It ain't fittin' for no little white girl to call a nigger that."

"But, you're older than me. My Daddy says to show respect to my elders by callin' 'em Ma'am."

"Baby girl, you can stop and listen anytime; I'll make sure don't nobody bother you. Say, ain't you one of Mister Ray's little girls?"

"Yes Maam; you know him?"

"Sure I do, lots of folks in the Quarters work for him; includin' my ole man. He be 'bout the nicest white man I know. Here, this will help you cool off a little, honey. Sit down on this step in the shade and enjoy yo' self. Just leave the bottle there when you're done and I'll come out later and get it."

Jo thanked her and settled down on the step to enjoy her windfall; she had hardly taken a sip of her cold drink when Aunt Bessie drove by and saw her. Aunt Bessie almost wrecked her car stopping it so fast. She rolled down the window and yelled,

"What in the world do you think you're doin', Nancy Jo?"

"It's Ok, Aunt Bessie; the waitress gave me the cold drink and said I could sit here."

"It ain't OK. You get in this car right now!"

Jo sat the bottle down, walked over to the car, and opened the door; Aunt Bessie leaned across the seat, grabbed her arm and jerked her inside. Shaking a finger in Jo's face, she yelled, "You know better than that. You can't be hangin' around here! Just look at you in those short shorts that hardly cover your backside; what will people think. Besides, there's no tellin' what could happen if one of them drunks took it in his head to get hold of you."

"Aunt Bessie, those folks ain't drunk, they're just havin a good time listenin' to the music and dancing. They won't hurt me 'cause they're all nice folks. Anyway, they know I'm Mister Ray's girl and my Daddy don't mind that I'm over here."

"Your Daddy 'don't mind' that you walk home this way but he sure don't know that you stop and lollygag around no nigger honky tonk; I can tell you that much. Lord have mercy girl, your Daddy is gonna have a fit when he hears about this."

Bessie drove Jo home and walked with her into Ray's shop. "Ray, you won't believe what I caught this one doin' over in the Quarters."

Ray listened politely while she related where she found Jo and what she believed the problems to be. When she had finished, he calmly said, "Thank you for your concern Bessie. I'll take care of it."

After Bessie had driven off, Ray grinned at Jo, "Got caught enjoyin' the blues, did ya', Kiddo"? Don't worry; you're not in any trouble with me, but we do need to talk about it."

"Good, maybe you can tell me what put a bee in Aunt Bessie's bonnet."

"Honey, your Aunt Bessie is upset because she is a segregationist. Do you know what that is?"

"No, Daddy."

"It's folks who really, truly believe that niggers are fine as long as they stay in their place but that the two races should never, ever mix on any social or personal level. Honey, there's lots of folks around here feel this way, includin' many of our relatives, and I'm sure you'll hear more about their views over the years. You would be wise to listen to what they say, ask them questions and try to see why they think as they do. That's how you learn, and learnin' what folks think is a good thing 'cause it helps you understand their actions. Now, what I'm fixin' to tell you is very important, so listen carefully to what I'm sayin', after you have learned what other folks think, you have to develop your own thoughts and beliefs about niggers. Don't let Aunt Bessie or anyone else push their beliefs off on you. You make up your own mind on the subject and then do what you feel is right."

"But Daddy you don't think like Aunt Bessie; why didn't you tell her so?"

"You're right, I don't. Another thing you'll learn, as you get older, is you don't change other people's beliefs or way of thinkin' by insulting them or fightin' with them about it. Over time, some folks are goin' to change their segregationist way of thinkin' and some never will; either way, it's not your place to get in their face about it. Bessie loves you and she just wanted to be sure you were safe. You understand that?'

"Sure, Daddy, I know she loves me."

"It'll keep things more peaceful and save your Aunt Bessie a lot of worry if, next time you want to stop at the Blue Moon and listen to the music, you just go around back so she won't see you if she drives by."

CHAPTER 21

Ray Hires Sam Morton

Ray worked for many years with a black man, named Sam Morton, and they became good friends. Ray and Sam had much in common, they were both self-taught musicians who liked the same kinds of music, each was a skilled carpenter who enjoyed working with wood, and many of their values and beliefs about God, mankind, and politics were the same.

Sam's route home from work took him directly passed Ray's house; hence, Ray often asked Sam to "drop by on your way home so you can see what I'm working on and maybe give me a hand".

Sam was the proud owner of an old pick up truck, and occasionally he volunteered its use to deliver lumber or other heavy material to Ray's house. Sometimes he brought his wife, Vera, with him when he made these deliveries.

If Grace happened to be in the yard when Sam drove up with Vera, she would wander over to the truck to pass the time with Vera or invite her into the yard to look at some flower or shrub that was growing there. It soon became clear that Grace and Vera were kindred spirits. They shared a love for gardening, a dry sense of humor and a real passion for fishin'. Both couples felt a little sad that these short visits were the extent of social contact acceptable between them.

One evening, as he sat drinking after supper coffee, Ray exclaimed, "Shorty, I've figured it out."

"That's good but just what did you figure out, Archie?"

"How I can have Sam over here more often without gettin' folks upset or creatin' a dangerous situation."

"Ok, let's hear it."

"I'm gonna hire him as a handyman. As long as the neighbors believe he's hired help, nobody will wonder why he is here so much."

"Can't we hire Vera, too? Folks know that Leona worked for me 'til she had those twins and quit, so they won't think anything of me hirin' Vera. Really, Archie, I can use help on wash day and I bet she would like the idea of earning a little extra money."

"Grace, I can't afford to really hire Sam. We just don't have enough money to pay somebody to do things that I'm perfectly able to do. My plan is to have Sam help me with my projects and, in return, he can bring some of his projects over here so I can help him. The handyman ruse is just a cover story so we can spend more time together."

"Well, I really need help with the laundry. Since Leona quit, the kids have been real good about pickin' up the slack but they're startin' to get pretty tired of it. Can't we offer to pay Vera the same money that I was payin' Leona?"

"Sure, if you don't think she'll be insulted."

"Thanks Archie, I know I can put it to her in such a way that she won't be insulted."

So Sam and Vera were hired. The first project Ray and Sam did was to convert the huge garage at the end of the back lawn into a workshop and, adjacent to it, they constructed a nice big laundry room for Grace and Vera.

Hiring the Mortons allowed Ray and Grace to pursue a wonderful friendship; and, observing the relationship between their parents and the Mortons gave the kids a great lesson in race relations.   The kids often found Grace and Vera bare foot, with their jeans rolled up above their knees, laughing over some shared joke while they did laundry; some times they found them shelling peas on the back porch or drinking coffee in the kitchen while good naturedly arguing about the best fishin' hole.

One afternoon when Jo came home from school, she discovered Grace and Vera dancing to a recording of some wonderful delta blues; "Wow, that's a good song. Did you buy us a new record?"

Grace and Vera immediately stopped dancing, turned, saw Jo and embarrassedly sat down at the kitchen table; Grace, rather breathlessly responded to Jo, "No Honey, I didn't buy this record, Vera gave it to us. It's a record of a man that Sam knows."

"Wow, really, Sam knows somebody who can sing and play the blues that good?"

"Yes, he does." Grace laughed; "You know, Sam's a pretty good musician himself and he jams with lots of different folks around here."

"Boy howdy, Sam's lucky; is that man singin' somebody famous?"

Vera answered, "He's just an ole nigger called Mississippi John Hurt; he mostly sings and plays pretty close to his home. Sam met him in the Delta awhile back. I wouldn't say he's famous, but he's sure good, ain't he?"

Mimicking her Daddy Jo exclaimed, "Hell, he's better than good.'"

Grace burst out laughing, then got herself under control enough to say in a stern tone, "Jo you know better than to talk like that." Then, stifling a giggle, Grace offered a deal; "If you don't tell your Daddy or Sam about our dancin' I won't tell about you cussin'."

"Deal, but Daddy don't care if you dance."

"I know that, but if he and Sam ever heard about Vera and me doin' a hoochy-coochy in the kitchen and gettin' caught by one of the kids, they would tease us to death."

"Yeah, I reckon they would."

The kids liked to hang around the workshop watching Ray and Sam work with the power tools or listening to them give an impromptu concert, with Sam playing the guitar and Ray on the mouth harp.

Ray loved to whistle and could whistle the most complex and intricate musical pieces with a pitch that was always right on and tones that were hauntingly beautiful. Sam enjoyed whistling, though he was not as good at it as Ray. The neighbors often enjoyed hearing the two of them whistle a duet while they worked in the shop.

The Morton's son, Lonnie, was about Cary's age and they often brought him when they came to the Simmons. This caused no raised eyebrows since it was pretty much accepted that niggers were too poor to afford baby sitters.   Cary and Lonnie became buddies and spent many pleasant afternoons in Cary's room playing with his electric train set, reading comics and just goofing off or hanging around the shop with Ray and Sam.

CHAPTER 22

More "Ladies" of the Church

Lilly Ann gave birth to one son early in her marriage; she wanted a large family and did nothing to prevent bearing more children. However, her second and third sons, were not born until she was well into her 40's and the oldest son was in college. She was an experienced and devoted mother to her two young sons, acting as "room mother", running the PTA, and becoming a dedicated youth leader at the Tannerville Baptist Church.

Lee Ann had a special place in her heart for Ray. She was ten years older than Ray, and had fond memories of how, as a baby and a young child, his face lit up with a big smile whenever he saw her. She took him almost everywhere she went; their mother said that she "spoiled that boy rotten", but Lilly Ann paid her no mind and continued to give him special attention.

The bond between brother and sister was strong and he was happy living so near her. She loved Ray's kids and included them in all the school and church functions that she attended.

Ever since the 'ladies of the church' in North Le Grande had treated Sarah so viciously, embarrassed his Mother and hurt his kids, Ray avoided churches like the plague. However, he believed that his kids would benefit from spending time with their Aunt Lilly Ann. He also felt that being active in a church where they were welcomed with open arms would undo some of the damage inflected by those vicious 'ladies of the church' in North Le Grande; so he encouraged them to accept their Aunt's invitations.

His theory proved correct; soon the kids were attending Sunday school regularly and becoming involved in lots of church related activities - the Children's Choir, Royal Ambassadors, Girls Auxiliary, and Vacation Bible School. Even though the kids enjoy these activities, they never pass up a chance to go fishin' with their parents. They gladly skip any activity that conflicts with fishin'.

One evening, while Grace was away visiting her father and Ray was working in his shop, a group of 'ladies of the church' came to call. As soon as he saw them open the gate to his yard, Ray walked out of the shop and greeted them, "Evenin' ladies, Grace is not home and I'm working on a project out here in the shop. Is there something I can do for ya'll?"

Now, Ray knew good and well that this was not gentlemanly behavior and that good manners dictated he invite the ladies up onto the porch and offer them some ice tea or a cold drink. However, he also knew that the ladies were on a mission to get him to attend church; which he had no intention of doing. He figured if they had to stand around his yard while they talked, they would give up sooner and he could get back to the work in his shop.

The deacon's wife gave Ray a stiff, phony smile that didn't reach her eyes and spoke in a syrupy sweet voice. "Ray, we sure enjoy secin' your precious children in church so often with their Aunt Lilly Ann."

"Well, Maude, they seem to enjoy it and Lilly Ann sure likes havin' them go with her; so Shorty and I figure it can't do 'em any harm." Ray gave her a devilish grin as he spoke.

The ladies gasped and, after a short pause, one of them gave a nervous giggle. "Oh go on Ray, you know it ain't nice to talk like that. I think you are just trying to tease us."

"Could be." Ray answered dryly.

Maude, the deacon's wife, was a persistent woman and not about to let Ray's good looks or charming grin distract her or put her off from her mission, so she tried again. "We sure would like to have you and Grace join us in fellowship on Sunday. We think it would be good for ya'll and your children if you did. You know, they say 'the family that prays together stays together'."

"I don't know who they are but Shorty and I say 'the family that fishes together stays together'."

Ray's flip response produced more nervous giggles from the ladies and angered Maude.

"Now Ray, you know that fishin' on Sunday goes against everything we Southern Baptists believe in and taking the kids with you; why that's just teaching them to sin." Maude lectured, while the ladies, trying to look solemn, nodded their agreement.

"Ya'll must not know that I'm a Southern Agnostic and I believe that fishin' anytime you can, even on Sunday, is good for the soul." Ray shot back with a chuckle.

"Well, I never!" Maude huffed, spun around and barked an order to the ladies. "Come on! Let's go before I say something that the Good Lord won't forgive me for."

As they marched away, Ray could be heard softly whistling 'Onward Christian Soldiers' under his breath.

This caused Maude to mutter "Heathen!" just loud enough for Ray to hear.

Feeling that Maude's sarcastic remark was not a very Christian thing, one of the braver ladies challenged her. "Really, Maude, don't you think maybe that's uncalled for? You can show a little respect even if you don't agree with his religion."

Maude jerked around and glared at her accuser. "What on earth are you talking about?"

With Maude glaring at her, the lady lost her bravery fast. "I mean, it seems like he's of another faith and… well… after all… we show respect to the Catholics even though we know they're on the wrong road."

"Honestly, Sadie you're just too naïve for your own good. There ain't no such a religion as Southern Agnostic.", came Maude's caustic reply.

Cary got himself a paper route so he could earn some pocket money. His route included the Quarters; so, when he spent time there it was just assumed that he was having a hard time collecting the money due him for the papers. Most white folks believed that niggers were not only poor but also miserly. In actuality, Cary's black customers paid him more willingly and faithfully than many of his white customers.

The first Saturday that Cary tried to collect from a small house on the edge of the Quarters, a woman responded, "Come back tomarrah paperboy", in the sweetest voice he had ever heard; a throaty contralto reminded him of soft velvet or perhaps warm honey. After that, even though Cary knew that she preferred to pay on Sunday, he continued to stop by each Saturday just to hear her say in that wonderful voice, "Come back tomarrah paperboy". Eventually, Cary learned that she was a hooker, but this did nothing to diminish her in his eyes, he knew her to be a warm and gentle person who always paid her bill and took a few minutes to chat with him, unless she had company.

In a short time, most folks in the Quarters became aware that Cary was a friend of Lonnie Morton and accepted his presence anywhere that he chose to go. He often participated in games of sand lot baseball with the kids in the Quarters. It was through this activity that he met and became friends with Tony Mason, the younger brother of Frank Mason. Cary was very impressed by the fact that Frank, a fifteen year old, was already playing semi-professional baseball for the Le Grande Black Bears and that Tony hoped to do the same thing.

Cary regularly stopped in at the little grocery store in the Quarters to get a Nehi orange drink and cookies. The cookies sold in that store were homemade; plus, they were larger, tastier, and cheaper than any he could get elsewhere. Sometimes, on Sunday afternoons, he would join the Morton's at the church they attended. This church went full bore all day, not stopping at noon as the white churches did, and it featured music that was upbeat and joyous. It wasn't the sedate organ or piano music that he heard at the Baptist church that he attended with his Aunt Lilly Ann. Here they played trumpets, trombones, drums, tambourines, guitars as well as piano, and everyone sang & danced along with the music. Cary was amazed at the contrast between the two churches; he remarked to Miz Morton "y'all really make a joyful noise unto the Lord, that's for sure."

CHAPTER 23

Takin' Daddy's Lunch

Ray was promoted to Shipping Foreman at the mill; the new position required him to put in longer hours, attend management meetings, and do some traveling on behalf of the mill. He disliked spending less time with Grace and the kids; he managed to spend time with Grace late in the evenings but usually the kids were asleep before he got home. After a few weeks of seeing very little of the kids, Ray came up with a plan to correct this situation.

One morning at breakfast, he informed the kids "for the rest of the summer, you kids take turns bringing me a hot lunch at the mill."

Jo gave her Daddy a quizzical look and started gigglin'. This set Margaret Ann and Cary off and they burst into giggle fits; Grace was unable to resist the kids infectious gigglin' soon joined in. Ray, utterly confused by this reaction, asked, "Why is that so funny?"

"Daddy, you eat cold lunches all winter and now you want hot ones in the summer; that's silly."

"OK, its silly, but its what I want."

Cary considered this chore to be a privilege; and, when it was his turn to deliver Daddy's lunch; he happily rode his bike across town, over the railroad tracks, through Paper Mill Village, and waited for his Daddy to meet him at the fence by the loading dock. After delivering the lunch and talking with his Daddy for while, he was free to do as he pleased until suppertime.

One day as he was returning home from delivering lunch, Cary rode his bike through a wooded area between the paper mill and Paper Mill Village; here he discovered a group of black kids skinny-dipping in a pretty, little pond. This pond was not far from the road, but the trees and vines around it had grown so thick and close together that they created a secluded oasis. One of the black kids noticed Cary at the edge of the pond and called out, "Ain't you that white paperboy from the Quarters?"

"That's me", grinned Cary

Another kid said, "Don't y'all hang out some with Lonnie Morton?"

"Right again."

"Well, I reckon you're an OK white boy, so if you wanna join us, go ahead and shuck them drawers and hop in." Cary needed no further encouragement; he quickly stripped and jumped in the water. After that, Cary was always welcome at the pond and he spent many a pleasant afternoon with his new friends swinging, like Tarzan, from the vines surrounding the pond and frolicking in the water like a white fish among a school of brown ones.

On the rare occasion that any of his white pals asked where he had been all afternoon; he blew them off with, "Just piddling on the way back from taking my Daddy his lunch." This never caused much reaction because every southerner knows it's easy for a young boy to piddle away a summer afternoon when ever the chance arises.

Jo knew about the pond in the woods but instinctively avoided going there. If grown ups learned that a white boy was skinny-dipping with the niggers; it would likely be considered an excusable lapse in judgment caused by his youth and the temptation of cool water on a hot summer day. However, it would be a very different story if a white girl were to be discovered anywhere near the area; that would be a scandal of great proportions and, at the very least, would result in a severe scolding for the white girl and beatings for the black kids. This taboo was just another unpleasant fact of life and, as far as Jo was concerned, she didn't let it dampen her spirit any.

Jo was a happy natured child who let very few things upset her. More than once her Daddy had held her happy attitude toward life up as an example to a friend or relative. He would pull Jo close to his side and say, "Now this child has the right idea about life. If life gives her a lemon, she just makes lemonade."

Jo liked delivering Daddy's lunch because she knew that she would have his undivided attention focused on her for a little while and she gloried in that. She felt very grownup and special when he talked to her about his work and shared his knowledge of trains with her. He pointed out what type of engine each train had, how the boxcars were loaded, how they were coupled together, and where each train was headed.

Often Daddy would say, "Sit there on that log by the fence and keep me company while I eat" and she knew that something amusing had happened at the mill and he wanted to share it with her.

"You remember me telling you about Jimmy and how he's making things uncomfortable and tickin' off some of my crew with his bragging and trying to impress me all the time?"

Jo nodded.

"Well, it's gotten so bad that most of the crew are shunning him and looking at me as if to say 'are you taken in by this, are you?' This morning when I came out on the dock, Jimmy drove his forklift right up next to me and shouted, 'Loadin' this boxcar is shor' hard work Mister Ray but that's fine, jus fine. I luv hard work - the harder the better.'

Ray took a couple of bites of his lunch and continued; "This was the opening I'd been waitin' for and I used it to let him know that I was wise to his ways. I told him, 'Well, since you luv hard work so much, why don't you get down off that forklift and push them rolls of paper up onto the boxcar by hand?' Jimmy's eyes got big, his mouth fell open and the rest of the crew started grinning and laughing out loud. Now everybody, including Jimmy, knows that I'm wise to him."

One good thing to come from Ray's promotion was the improvement of the family's financial situation. They now had the means to buy a real family car – a late-model Willis Jeep station wagon. Prior to purchasing the Jeep, their only motor transportation was a very old Ford Coupe that had no back seat. The old Ford could accommodate a driver and one passenger but, by no means, could it be considered a family car. When Ray and Grace took the kids anywhere in the old Ford, Ray propped the trunk lid open with a two by four and the kids rode back there.

Ray and Grace celebrated owning a real family car by taking the kids on a trip to New Orleans. While in New Orleans they visited the Audubon Zoo, where Grace, with Jo following close behind, immediately headed to the area where the large jungle cats were housed.

When they arrived, there was a large group in front of the panther cage; children were making growling noises and clawing gestures, a little old lady was yelling "Here Kitty-Kitty" and a couple of teen-agers were trying to throw pop corn into the cage. All this activity was making the beautiful, sleek, black animal inside very agitated. The panther was pacing, snarling and switching its tail rapidly back and forth.

Grace eased around to the edge of the crowd and got as near the side of the cage as the barriers would allow. She waved her hand until the panther looked directly at her; she kept her eyes focused on the animal and began talking in a low, slow and soothing tone.

"It's OK, fella, I'd be mad too if folks acted like that in front of my house. You're a wonderful, beautiful, magnificent animal;

most of them don't often get to see anything as grand as you and they don't realize how you hate to be gawked at. Just look at me, stay calm and still. If you don't move or react to them, they'll soon get bored and go away".

Jo was standing quietly beside Grace and, to her utter amazement, the panther stopped pacing, kept looking at Grace, lay down on the floor of the cage and began to purr. Jo had no doubt that the panther understood what Grace was saying and she was sure that, if permitted, Grace could and would have entered the cage and scratched that big cat behind the ears, just like she did with their house cat at home.

CHAPTER 24

Harold Gets Tipsy

Ray needed someone to run errands and do some local pick-up and deliver work; he hired Harold, a fat, jolly, black man with a friendly, easygoing manner and slightly below average intelligence to do this job, and between deliveries, he was to keep the loading dock area swept and clear of debris.

Harold was very proud of his job, considered Ray to be the best boss in the world, and worked very hard at pleasing him.

Not long after Harold was hired, he had to deliver something to Ray at home. The house had two exterior doors, one on the east side and one on the north side. This arrangement of exterior doors presented a problem, for Harold; he couldn't tell which was the back door, so after a few moments of deliberation, he just knocked on the door closest to where he was standing. In response to Harold's knock, Grace came to the door; "Howdy Miz Simmons, I've got somethin' to deliver to Mister Ray."

"Hello Harold." Grace unlatched the screen and turned to go fetch Ray; "Come on in; I'll tell him you're here."

When Harold stepped inside, he knew that he had used the wrong door because he was in the parlor, not the kitchen. As soon as Ray entered the room, Harold blurted out, "I'm sorry Ray, I didn't know that was yo' front door that I knocked on". Realizing that he hadn't called Ray 'Mister', he began trying to apologize for that blunder as well.

Ray interrupted Harold with a grin and a shake of his head, "Relax Harold; no harm done; one door is as good as another and you don't have to call me Mister when there's nobody else around to get upset about it."

Harold was amazed at being admitted into the Simmons home through the front door and at the friendly way Ray and Grace talked to him, he had never had any white folks treat him this way before.

One evening, Harold was sitting with his friends at the Palm Club, a local beer joint; his drinking buddies started bragging about various deeds that they had done. Harold, not wanting to be left out, declared, "I'm real important over in the shipping department at the mill. In fact, I'm so important that I'm allowed to use Ray Simmons's front door and I don't have to call him 'Mister' neither."

Harold's drinking buddies didn't believe a word he was saying and they began teasing him about it.

"Harold, when you go over to your buddy Ray's place, does Grace serve tea to you?" One of them jokingly inquired.

Harold, not understanding that the fellow was poking fun at him, replied, "No; but one time she did give me some left over pound cake to take home and eat with my supper."

"Ooh! Left over pound cake; that makes you almost family, don't it?"

"I think you're makin' it all up, Harold. I bet you ain't ever even been to Mister Ray Simmons's house."

By now, Harold was pretty tipsy and getting' frustrated by all the teasing. "Come on," he said, "We'll go over there right now and I'll prove it."

A couple of Harold's buddies drove him over to Ray's house; Harold got out of the car, sauntered up to the front door and said in a loud voice, "Ray, are ya'll home?"

The minute Ray heard Harold's loud voice and the way he was slurring his words, it became obvious to him that Harold was three sheets to the wind and not thinking straight. Quickly sizing up the situation, Ray opened the front door, pulled Harold inside and addressed him in a low, but firm, voice.

"Harold, listen carefully to me and answer quietly. Are you trying to prove something to your buddies out in that car?"

Harold grinned crookedly at Ray. "Shor am, Ray."

Ray now spoke very firmly. "Harold, you're drunk and you're puttin' yourself, me, and my family in a bad situation. Now, tell me what you're doin' here."

Harold was beginning to sober up enough to realize that he could be in trouble; he shook his head a little to clear it and tried to explain about the bragging at the bar.

Ray understood enough of what Harold was saying to formulate a plan. "Alright, Harold, there's been no harm done yet, but you've got to listen to me real good and do as just I say, otherwise we may ruffle some feathers and get the neighbors riled up. Are you with me on this, Harold?"

Sobering rapidly, Harold hung his head in shame. "Yes sir, I understand, I'm real sorry about messin' up like this; I'll do whatever y'all say, Mister Ray."

Ray told him. "I won't embarrass you in front of your friends; so here's what we're gonna do."

After telling Harold his plan, Ray and Harold walked out into the front yard, shook hands and in a voice loud enough for the nearby neighbors to here, Ray said, "Thanks for takin' the time to deliver that stuff, Harold; I really needed it. You enjoy what's left of the evenin' and tell your friends that I appreciate them drivin' you over here. I'll see you at work tomorrow."

"OK, Boss. Glad to help, see y'all in the mornin'." Harold answered, as he walked away and got in the car.

By pretending that Harold had come to his house on business, Ray was able to defuse the situation. The mill ran three shifts and Ray had no telephone in his home, so it was not unusual for mill hands, black as well as white, to come to Ray's home in the evening if there was a problem at the mill. The ingenious part of Ray's charade was having Harold use the term 'boss', instead of 'Mister'; by doing this Ray had allowed Harold to save face with his buddies.

When Harold got home, completely sobered up and realized exactly what had occurred, he was very grateful to Ray and vowed never to make a mistake like that again.

CHAPTER 25

A Day of Fishin

At supper on Friday evening, Ray asked Grace, "Aren't you goin' to help your sister move into her new place tomorrow?"

"That's the plan. I reckon you're gonna be over to the mill and Margaret Ann is going to the beach with Nelly's family; so I asked Bessie to keep an eye on Jo and Cary and feed them lunch."

"Surprisin' as it may seem, I don't have to go to the mill tomorrow; I was thinkin' of getting' up a fishin' trip."

"Darn! I really can't back out on Doris at the last minute, but I'm sure Jo and Cary will want to go with you?"

"Aw, I don't think they like fishin' that much." Ray said just loudly for Jo and Cary, who were at the sink washing and drying the dishes to hear. He winked at Grace and continued, Maybe, I'll see if Wilton wants to go."

Jo responded just as Ray knew that she would. "Oh Daddy, don't be silly; you know that we both love fishin' and want to go."

"Y'all wouldn't rather hang out here and have Bessie watch you?"

"No way", Cary shook his head,"we're goin' with you."

On Saturday morning, Grace got up real early and packed a picnic while Ray hitched his old aluminum boat to the back of the Jeep; then he loaded the lunch, fishin' gear, and the kids into the Jeep. "OK kids, let's head out to Choctaw Creek and get the big 'uns; maybe Shorty will cook up fish and Hush Puppies for supper when we all get home this evenin'.

They drove the few miles to Choctaw Creek and pulled into the launch area nearest the highway. Jo unloaded their lunch, bait and fishin' gear while Ray and Cary unhitched and launched the boat. When the food, drinks and fishin' gear were stowed, they got into the boat and shoved off for a favorite fishin' spot about five miles up creek.

The boat was equipped with an outboard motor; however, Ray seldom used it. The river followed a meandering route with many twists and blind turns; it was full of Cypress knees, submerged vines and all manor of swamp debris that could damage a boat propeller. Additionally, Ray felt that churning up the water with a noisy motor was discourteous to the anglers who preferred to fish from the creek banks.

Jo took a seat in the left rear of the boat, Cary sat in the right rear, and their Daddy got in up front so that he could rig the poles while they paddled. For a while, Cary and Jo matched paddle strokes and kept the boat mid stream; away from the submerged snags that they knew lined the banks.

After a little while, Cary, feeling happy and full of mischief, decided to tease his sister a bit. He was the stronger of the two, and could easily out row his sister; so he impishly paddled harder; this causes the boat to move toward the left bank. While he was doing this, Cary kept a sharp eye on his Daddy to see if he was aware of what was going on. Ray gave no indication that he noticed anything amiss, so Cary grinned and took a rest while Jo paddled the boat back to mid-stream. Feeling smug that he had put one over on his sister and assuming that his Daddy was too busy to notice, Cary paddled his sister into the bank two more times.

When the boat got off course for the third time, Ray casually said, "Jo, come up here and check the riggin' on your pole, I'll take your paddle for a minute."

Ray took Jo's paddle and without a word, he easily paddled the boat back mid stream; then he proceeded to paddle it way over toward the right bank, handed Jo her paddle and went back to riggin' the other poles while a chagrined Cary had to paddle hard to get the boat back mid stream.

On the way home that afternoon, Ray pulled into the parking area in front of the Indian Grove Drugstore. "Come on in with me kids, it's hot in the Jeep; y'all can cool off and look over the comic books at the front of the store while I go back to the pharmacy and check on Shorty's prescription."

As they entered the store, he ruffled Cary's hair, patted his shoulder and said, "Your old man is sharper than he sometimes appears."

"How's that, Daddy?" Cary was expecting a tale about one of his Daddy's long ago fishin' trips; maybe the one where his Daddy had outsmarted an alligator, or perhaps he would hear, again, about the time that his Daddy had gotten lost in the swamp around Choctaw Creek and managed to find his way out with no compass.

Ray's reply took Cary by surprise. "I was wise to you the first time you pushed us off course this morning. I let it go on because your antics brought back good memories. I used to pull stunts like that on my sisters; besides, I figured the extra practice using a paddle wouldn't hurt Jo any. Just don't let me catch you trying to take advantage of your sister like that again, OK?"

"Yes Sir, I didn't mean no harm; I was just teasing her."

"I know that, son. I'm just pointin' out that sometimes a person will fake you out by not reactin' when they know darn well you are tryin' to put one over on them. If you get smug and too confident, you can set yourself up for problems. In the future, just assume that the other fellow is at least as smart as you are and I think you'll be OK."

"Gotcha'" Cary responded.

"Alright, I'm treating us all to an ice cream soda; Jo because she worked so hard at paddling; you because I think you learned a bit about human nature today and me 'cause I feel like celebrating an enjoyable days fishin'."

CHAPTER 26

Punishment

The house next to the Simmons', on the opposite side from Lilly Ann's, belonged to the Crenshaw family; Mr. Crenshaw worked at the mill. He and his wife had their hands full trying to provide for and raise their four rambunctious boys, all of whom were full of mischief.

One evening as the Simmons siblings were sitting on their shady back stoop enjoying the long summer twilight and a cold glass of Kool-Aid, the back screen door of the Crenshaw's house banged open and Roy Gene Crenshaw raced out at full speed, crying "Momma, please don't whoop me. I won't ever do it again!"

On his heels came his mother, waving a leather strap and screaming, "Roy Gene, you stop this minute. The more I have to chase you, the harder you're gonna' get it!!"

The Simmons kids watched and listened in fascination as Roy Gene ran around the house, through the front door and disappeared inside the house with his heavyset mother puffing along after him. The windows of the house were open, and the evening air carried the sounds from inside the house.

"Get out from under that bed and I mean right now!"

"I didn't mean to do it – I'm sorry – please let me off with a warning this time – Momma, don't whoop me."

This exchange was followed by the sound of a leather strap hitting a small bottom and a young boy yelling, between sobs; "Momma, please, stop – I'll be good - that hurts – please stop – I hate you."

When the commotion next door died down, Margaret Ann said, "I'm sure glad that Daddy and Grace don't punish us that way, aren't ya'll?"

Jo was quick to agree with her sister. "Boy, I'll say! That's embarrassing".

"Hurts too" Cary stated the obvious.

After a few minutes, Margaret Ann asked, "What do y'all hate the most about being punished?"

"I hate bein' grounded and havin' to stay in my room. They won't even let me play with my electric train when I'm stuck in there." Cary quickly answered.

"I hate bein' fined and loosin' part of my allowance." Jo had recently discovered 'accessorizing' and spent hours every Saturday at Woolworth Five & Dime picking out hair barrettes and costume jewelry; so any reduction in funds really got to her.

Margaret Ann laughed at their answers, thinking they had both failed to mention the thing she hated most. "Know what I really, really hate the worst?" Without waiting for a response, she continued. "When Daddy gives me a 'good talkin' to'. You know, he gets that sad, hurt look in his eyes and he starts out 'I'm more disappointed than I am mad.' Then, toward the end of the talk, he says 'Can you just tell me why you did it?' and leans back in his chair. You know, he sits there like he's fully expectin' you to explain your actions. So you sit there squirming, trying to think of somethin' sensible to say and after a long time all you can come up with is 'I don't know. I just did' or somethin' stupid like that."

Jo and Cary nodded in unison because they knew exactly how she felt; a dozen spankings would be less painful than enduring the look of the disappointment and hurt in their Daddy's eyes while he sat reasoning with them and trying to point out 'the error of their ways'.

CHAPTER 27

The Dragon Picture, Again

Rumblings of dissatisfaction with segregation were beginning in the Deep South. For the first time in her life Jo heard folks, black and white, talking and publicly debating about how The Negro should be treated in a more fair and humane manner. Indeed, a few brave white folks even suggested that they be treated as an equal. This was not yet a popular view and segregationists insisted that the only ones who expressed it were bleeding heart liberals; they kept assuring each other that no sane person would take the ranting of such nigger lovers seriously. They just kept on preaching the 'segregation now and segregation forever' message loud, long, and often and insisting that everybody knew that the niggers down here in the south were happy with things as they were.

It was around this time that Miz Simmons began having dizzy spells, some so bad that she nearly passed out. Ray and Grace were concerned that she would become dizzy or disoriented in the night; they worried about her being alone and perhaps unable to summon any help.

Grace pondered, "We really need somebody to stay with your momma at night."

Ray agreed; "I know we do but you know how Momma is, she'd think we'd lost our mind if we suggested she couldn't take care of herself."

Ray and Grace wondered aloud if any neighbor might stay with her.

"Miz Velma? - No, when Sam gets on a drunk she has her hands full trying to deal with her errant husband."

"Miz Polk? - No way, she dips snuff and keeps spitting into an old coffee can and, as a reformed dipper, Momma finds that repulsive."

"Cora Lee? - Lord no! She's the scandal of the neighborhood the way she's busy most nights with all those men in and out. The whole neighborhood is tryin' to figure out if she is sellin' moonshine or her favors"

After excluding the neighbors, they turned to family and Grace suggested; "Well, how about we move one of the kids in with her for awhile? She loves them to death and misses havin' them live next door to her."

"That could work." Ray agreed; he saw no reason why one of his kids shouldn't do this. "How about Margaret Ann?"

"No, she is just beginnin' to make new friends and get involved in high school activities. That's real important to a teenager and we can't ask her to give that up."

"Ok, maybe Cary?"

"Not hardly; Ray, he's still a little boy and has already had too many changes in his young life. I don't want to even consider another change for him right now." Cary was growing up fast but Grace still saw him as her baby and wasn't ready to have him out of the nest, even temporarily, no matter how good the reason.

"Well that leaves Jo. How do you think she will react if we ask her to do it?"

"She might like it, especially having a bedroom to herself. The room she and Margaret Ann share is pretty small and sometimes they get on each others nerves."

So it was determined that Jo would stay with her Grandma Simmons for one school term.

On a rainy, fall afternoon shortly after Jo moved in with her Grandma, she became bored and restless. Because of the rain, she couldn't go outside; she didn't want to go in the kitchen and help Grandma shell peas; homework held no appeal, and she wasn't even enjoying the book that she'd been reading. Looking around, spotted an old trunk and on this rainy afternoon, it promised to provide her a welcome distraction.

Many times, Jo had watched her Grandma go to this trunk and pull out some treasure from the past. She knew it held some of her Daddy's old report cards, the gloves her Grandma wore on her wedding day, newspaper clippings, and some old photographs. She was curious about what else it might hold; excitedly, she opened the trunk and began examining its contents. Way down at the bottom of the trunk, separate from all the other photographs, she came across a faded old group photo.

Having seen pictures and drawings of Ku Klux Klan members in her schoolbooks, she knew immediately that she held a 'Klan' picture in her hand and was really intrigued by it.

From time to time, Jo had overheard snatches of conversation between family members that lead her to suspect that her late Grandpa Simmons had been a Klan sympathizer or maybe even a member. Knowing how her Daddy felt about judging anyone by the color of their skin, it was hard to reconcile him being raised by anyone who was a racial bigot; so, she pretty much concluded that she had misunderstood those bits of conversation.

Now her imagination began to run wild. Perhaps Grandpa had been very foolish in his youth and joined the Klan on a dare, but surely, he never took part in anything bad that they did - It could be he really hated the Klan and had sneaked into one of their meetings, and, hoping to expose them, he had secretly taken this picture. Jo was sure that her Grandma would tell her all about it; so, in anticipation of a good family story, she took the picture into the kitchen to ask Grandma about it.

"Grandma, how did this Klan picture get in your trunk? Do we know who's in it?"

Miz Simmons turned abruptly and gave Jo a stern look; when she spoke, her voice had an angry tone that Jo had never heard her use before. "I declare child, you're too nosey for your own good. Put that thing back in there and don't meddle in my stuff again!! - It's just a picture of some people I used to know – that's all – PUT IT AWAY and go do your homework."

This out of character reaction surprised Jo and hurt her feelings but, after pouting for a while, she found something else to do and put the incident out of her mind. Except for this one incident, Jo's stay with Grandma was very pleasant, and both of them were a little sad when Jo moved back home.

CHAPTER 28

Beau Williams

Each Fourth of July, the city of Wilsonville held a huge celebration in the park. There were all kind of fun things to do, you could cool off in the swimming pool, gorge on hot dogs, RC Colas and Moon Pies, or try to win a Cupie Doll at one of the carnival booths. There were loads of things going on at the ball field; there was a hog-calling contest, and a greased pig chase, or you could try climbing a greased pole to get the twenty-dollar bill off the top. For folks who liked music or were into politics, the bandstand was the place to be;

here you could listen to live music and hear local, county and a few minor state officials talk about what they would do if they were elected or re-elected.

During one Fourth of July celebration, Jo happened by the bandstand while a young girl was singing a hillbilly tune; this little girl had a big beautiful voice that held Jo mesmerized. Jo worked her way to the very front of the crowd and around to the front of the bandstand so she could see and hear better.

At the end of the performance, one of the politicians jumped off the bandstand and began 'pressing the flesh', as politicians everywhere like to do. Not being a shy child, Jo approached this politician and asked; "Hey Mister, you know that singer?"

The man turned to her with a warm, friendly smile. "Why sure I do, little lady; want to meet to her?"

His calling her 'little lady' made Jo feel very grown up and she liked him immediately. "Gosh, yeah, I sure do. I might be a singer someday, too"

"Well, just wait right over yonder under that big oak tree; I'll be back directly and take you up to meet her."

Jo hung around the big oak tree for what seemed to her a very long time; she was just about to give up on meeting the singer when the man came back and took her hand. "Come on, little lady, lets go talk to that singer."

"I thought you forgot me."

"No ma'am", the man answered in a booming voice, intentionally made loud enough to be heard by the crowd near the bandstand. "I always remember and I always keep every promise I make. I'm Beau Williams, but you can call me Beau."

Jo stammered; "Oh no Sir, I can't call you that; my Daddy would skin my hide; he says I have to call grown men Mister, so I'll just call you Mister Williams, if that's OK with you."

"That's just fine, honey; you should always do what your Daddy tells you. Now tell me who you are so I can properly introduce you."

"I'm Nancy Jo Simmons."

After introducing her to each member of the band, he approached the singer. "Say howdy to my new friend Nancy Jo

Simmons. She sure likes your singing and she might be a singer someday, too."

"Pleased to meet ya'll. What kind of singin' ya'll do?"

"Well, mostly just church choir and glee club stuff, but some folks say I'm pretty good."

Jo and the singer spent a few more minutes chatting; then, the singer excused herself to go change her costume.

Jo's benefactor led her off the bandstand, shook her hand, told her that he was glad to have made her acquaintance, and he hoped they would meet again someday.

Jo had never been on a bandstand before; had never talked to a professional entertainer, and it was the first time a grown man had shook her hand or treated her in such a courtly grown up manner; thus, she was greatly impressed by the whole experience and knew she would never forget Beau Williams.

CHAPTER 29

A Black Segregationist

Margaret Ann and Jo developed a casual friendship with two black kids whose house they passed every day on their way home from the high school. Pearl, a fat girl; mostly sat on her front porch drinking soda pop, eating Moon Pies and watching her younger brother, Leroy, practice his tap dancing skills on the sidewalk in front of their house; Leroy was a short skinny kid about eight or nine years old, he had a big friendly grin and a mouthful of very white teeth.

One day, as Margaret Ann and Jo were passing, Leroy did a very flashy series of steps, bowed, grinned broadly and asked; "Hey, white girls, y'all think I'm a good dancer?"

"We sure do, and we like watchin' you."

"Well, watch all you want. Right now, it's free 'cause I'm still learnin' but one day I'm gonna' be a famous dancer and then folks are gonna haf to pay to see me."

Margaret Ann and Jo laughed and continued on their way.

Jo chuckled, "You know, I wouldn't be at all surprised if his prediction comes true, he's really a good dancer."

After Leroy broke the ice that day, the kids would call greetings to each other; sometimes Margaret Ann and Jo would stop for a few minutes to watch Leroy dance.

One day Pearl waddled down from the porch and started to talk with them about what they were studying in school. Almost immediately, her mother yelled from inside the house, "Pearl, you get back on this porch, right now. Don't let me catch you hanging on that fence talking to them white girls again, you hear?" Pearl shook her head in disgust; turned and went back up on her porch.

When Jo got home, she talked to Grace about the incident. "I wonder why Pearl's mother acted mean and embarrassed her own daughter like that."

Grace, wanting to help Jo understand, offered her view of the incident. "I suspect Pearl's mother shares your Aunt Bessie's belief that whites and blacks should stay in their own place. Honey, it's not just white folks who are segregationists; many black people feel the same way. When you run into anybody who feels that way, it's wise to accept their attitude because you aren't likely to change it. Maybe, from now on, you and Margaret Ann can just smile and wave at Pearl and Leroy and keep on walking. That way Pearl's mother won't get mad with ya'll, or with Pearl, OK?"

"OK, but I still don't understand why grown folks have to make things so complicated. All, I wanted to do was be nice to Pearl and Leroy; 'cause I like 'em."

Later that night, Grace shared, with Ray, details of the incident and Jo's resulting confusion; his response was, "Getting these kids raised isn't an easy job is it?"

"Why do you say that, Archie?"

"Don't you ever get the feeling that this kid rearing business is overwhelming? You know, feeling sort of afraid you'll preach at them too much and they'll tune out everything you say or you'll get so busy with small stuff that you leave out an important life lesson that you should be teaching them."

Grace's passionate response surprised Ray. "Boy, do I ever! I thought those feelings sprang from me never having had a child of my own; I kinda figured that rasin' my siblings and your kids was harder for me than it was for a real parent."

"That dog just don't hunt; hell, Shorty, you're about as real a parent as I have ever seen; you run rings around Sarah in that department."

"Really? I'm sure glad you told me that; but I'm real surprised at you doubtin' yourself. You're so good with the kids that I never suspected you had any doubts or worries about how to raise 'em."

"I worry a lot about all they've been through in the last few years. Until they started livin' with you and me, they had never known anything but Sarah's moodiness, our arguments, and me bein' gone most of the time. Maybe they thought that was a normal situation; maybe they resent me for practically stealin' them from Sarah."

"I'm sure they don't feel that way. Anyway, you know you really didn't have any other option; if you hadn't taken them, the juvenile authorities would have. Now, that would have been a real mess; one you may never have been able to straighten out."

"Your point is well taken."

"Do you reckon it'll get any easier as they get older?"

"Nope, I guess all we can do is keep at it and hope we're doin' it right."

"Yeah, but sometimes it's almost like tryin' to take a trip without a road map or good directions."

CHAPTER 30

The Town Character

Like most small southern towns, Tannerville had a local character; a tiny black woman called Lizzy; she could be seen almost daily, shuffling around town wearing dirty, ill fitting shoes and layer upon layer of old, musty smelling, clothing - no matter what the season. Her hair was always in disarray, she carried a big stick in her hand, and alternated between muttering softly to herself and yelling, unintelligibly, at those that she encountered.

The first time Cary saw Lizzy, he was walking home from school with a group of neighborhood kids; as they saw Lizzy approaching, they began to giggle and push each other, one of them yelled, "Crazy lady comin', run for your life.", and they all ran, except Cary. He stood in the middle of the sidewalk, puzzled by what was happening around him, until a couple of the kids came back, grabbed his hand, and pulled him along with them.

When the group stopped to catch their breath, Cary, totally confused by this entire episode, demanded, "What's goin on? How come y'all are runnin' like that?"

"That's Lizzy; she's a crazy lady that lives over by the tracks in Paper Mill Village."

"She sure dresses funny. How come y'all say she's crazy and carry on like that when y'all see her?"

"Everybody knows about Lizzy. Ain't y'all's Daddy or Aunt Lilly Ann told you about her?"

"Naw, they never said nothin'."

"Her son was killed by a train, a long time ago, and it drove her crazy." One kid announced.

Another kid picked up the story; "Yeah. Every day she waits out by the tracks in front of her house for the six o'clock train – that's the one that killed her boy; then, she takes that old stick she carries and when the train is up even with her she begins screamin' and beatin' the train until the very last car had passed."

"Has she ever hurt anybody that y'all know of?"

"Nope, but she's so weird that we're all afraid that she might."

"Well that ain't much of a reason for y'all to act all goofy when you see her."

Cary was a very tenderhearted young boy. After noticing how mean most folks treated Lizzy, he felt sorry for her and would nod and say "Hi, Miss Lizzy" if he encountered her.

One Saturday morning a group of kids, including Cary, were in a little grocery store near the Quarters, when Lizzy walked in. All the kids, except Cary, ran from the store yelling "Crazy lady!!" Cary remained where he was and selected the cookie he wanted to purchase. As he approached the counter to pay for it,

Lizzy rushed passed him, pushed money into the store clerk's hand, and pointed to Cary's cookie.

The clerk said, "She wants to buy you that cookie."

Cary looked directly at her, smiled and accepted her gift with a cheery, "Thank you Miss Lizzy".

Lizzy beamed, and Cary was sure that he saw a gleam of happiness, mixed with a hint of pride in her eyes as she walked out of the store humming to herself.

That evening Cary relayed the incident to his Daddy.

"I'm glad to see you beginin' to understand some of what I've been tryin' to teach you." Ray's face displayed a proud grin.

Cary was puzzled by the remark. "How so?"

"Lizzy's very different from anybody you've met before, isn't she?"

Cary considered the question dumb; he was disappointed in his Daddy for asking it; hence, his response was slightly sarcastic. "Well, of course she is. You don't see very many short, skinny, black ladies who dress funny. On top of that Lizzy doesn't smell good and she acts loco most of the time; I mean, talkin' to herself, yellin' and beatin' trains and all that stuff; but she don't hurt nobody, and most of the time she seems to understand and like it when I say 'Hi' to her."

"I'm real proud of you, son, you've managed to see beyond all her differences and recognize in her a soul that responds to basic human kindness and respect. It's real easy to judge a person too quickly and to treat those who appear different in a rude or disrespectful manner."

Ray wanted to let Cary know his sarcastic tone hadn't gone unnoticed; so, after a short pause, he added, "By disrespectful, I'm talkin' about stuff like being sarcastic to an elder who asks what, in your opinion, is a dumb question. It's much wiser to judge slowly and to treat folks in a kind and respectful manner; unless, of course, the person has given you a really good reason not to."

Cary was chagrinned, gave his Daddy a sheepish look, he nodded his understanding and muttered an embarrassed, "Sorry, Daddy".

CHAPTER 31

Ray's Inventions

By the early 1950's, the paper company held patents on over thirty of Ray's inventions. He had invented an egg carton that opened in the middle; this design increased the speed with which assembly line workers could pack eggs into the carton. Another of his inventions, small treated paper cubes, that served as individual cream holders, was well received by the restaurant industry and the airlines because it was cheaper and easier to use than the little glass cream containers that restaurants had used prior Ray's invention.

The paper company patented most of Ray's designs, so that competing manufacturers couldn't copy them; moreover, they used many of them to improve production throughout their own mills. One such design was an attachment at the end of the 'bag line'; this attachment used forced air to make it easier for the ladies on that assembly line to lift, wrap and tie large bundles of bags. In addition, Ray re-designed the pulp machines so that they could extract the water and chemicals from the pulp three times faster than had ever been done before. Executives at the paper company were so impressed with this that they dubbed the newly designed machines, "The Simmons", in Ray's honor.

Of all Ray's inventions, the one in which he took the most pride was an air table used to re-direct huge, heavy stacks of 4' square poster-paper. The stacks – some 6' high – traveled from the production room down a metal-roller track until they reached a platform, there they stopped, and an operator manually re-directed them to one of three finishing rooms; depending on type and color, the stacks were sent left, right, or straight to be cut and packaged. This task required considerable physical effort for the operator to over-come the inertia of the now-still stack and the friction of the rollers – not to mention the cumbersome effort of mechanically manipulating the platform.

Ray's invention, a metal table with dozens of small holes in the top; through which air was forced at a great velocity; this air table replaced the old, manually controlled platform. Once the stack came to rest, floating on a thin layer of air, it was practically effortless for the operator to push the huge, heavy stack left, right or straight onto the proper track.

In late 1953, Ray, perfected yet another of his inventions and submitted it to corporate headquarters for consideration. Since the company had already patented so many of his inventions, he felt confident that this one would be well received. His latest invention was a process that made it possible to mass-produce paper milk cartons, with pour spouts, efficiently and profitably.

This was quite a revolutionary concept. Up to now, the only paper milk cartons being mass-produced were small, half pint or pint, containers with no pour spouts. These containers had a hole near the top into which the user inserted a straw and drank milk directly from the carton.

Glass was still the only practical packaging for large quantities of milk. The costs associated with packaging and distributing milk in glass containers was extremely high and the problems with them were well documented; they were awkward to handle and store; their frequent breakage resulted in massive loss of product and getting the containers returned for cleaning/sterilization was no easy task. The milk industry had been seeking a more cost effective packaging option for years. In fact, the industry had seen a couple of designs for paper containers that were strong enough to stand up to the storage and distribution process without rupturing; however, none could be mass-produced, nor did they provide any effective way to remove the milk from the container. Ray's carton, with its pour spout, made removing milk from them a snap, and his process for cost effective mass-production could easily make expensive glass containers obsolete. The only down side, that Ray could see, was the need for some special machinery to produce this type of container. Ray feared the corporate brass might balk at putting money into machinery to produce an unproven product.

CHAPTER 32

The 'N' Word

Integration had become a major political issue; in the Deep South, tension between the races was intensifying, and Jo was upset and mystified at what was occurring around her. She continued to smile and wave to her black friends when she saw them in the back of the bus; however, she was becoming increasingly uncomfortable doing so because some of them had begun to glare at her, instead of smiling and waving back. She avoided hanging out at The Field because it seemed that when black kids and white kids happened to be in The Field at the same time, they spent more time calling each other ugly names and throwing rocks at each other than they did enjoying a 'pick up' game of tag or baseball.

Recently, Jo had spoken to a young girl, in the Quarters, "I think that Sidney Poitier is a great Negro actor, don't you?"

The girl had given her a mean look and said, "He ain't no 'Negro'. He is a "Black – with a big B." With that flip remark, the girl walked off and left Jo standing there shocked and surprised.

Jo wanted to understand what was happening and she began reading every newspaper or magazine article that she could find about integration. She was shocked to read, in one newspaper, that it was no longer acceptable to use the word Negro; calling a black person a Negro was now considered almost as insulting as calling them nigger. The paper informed readers that everyone should now use the word "Black, with a capitol B".

Jo considered things already too tense between the races, and this confusing hubbub over a word wasn't going to help. She now understood how Daddy felt about the word nigger; it was going to be extremely hard for her to change. She meant no disrespect by using the word Negro, as she had been taught, and knew that any attempt to switch from the word Negro to the word Black would sound stiff and phony. Another thing about this word situation puzzled her; in the article that she read, the author said to use "the word Black, with a capitol B". She wondered just what he meant by that phrase; was one actually expected to say the entire phrase? If not, how did you indicate you were using a 'capitol B'? She resented the feelings of self-consciousness and insecurity that were bubbling inside of her and sometimes she got just plain mad at the whole world over it.

Jo was no saint, occasionally, rather than argue with her white friends, she would nod her head to indicate agreement when they were complaining about the niggers. On a few occasions, she had used the word nigger, just to fit in with the crowd. After doing this, she always felt guilty, cowardly and mean spirited.

What she didn't yet understand was that these feelings were not caused by the word itself, rather they resulted from her not being true to her beliefs. Truth be known, she had no complaint about Negro's in general; and, if it weren't a taboo in her part of the world, she would have happily become good friends with many of the Negro's she knew.

She alternately resented and worried about the fact that Daddy used the work nigger so easily and that he saw no need to change it. She was confident that local black folks knew that her Daddy wasn't a racial bigot; she had never seen any of them act in the least concerned when they heard him use that word. Yet, at times, it irritated her that he appeared to have little or no worry about this entire 'word' situation; especially when it was causing her so much worry and discomfort.

Another of Jo's major concerns was; many new black people had moved into the area and they seemed quick to take offence at any little thing a white person said or did. She had experienced their mean, sullen looks a few times and she suspected that they were just looking for any reason to pick a fight. She was afraid that one, or a group, of these newcomers might actually become violent if they heard her Daddy use the word nigger.

Jo's mind raced around in circles as she silently prayed. "Oh Dear Lord, it's just a word, worse than a lot of words, not as bad as some. Why do so many folks get all worked up over a word? Why do I let myself get so upset over that word; NO, not that word, the whole damned group of words - nigger, colored, Negro, Black, 'The Blacks', Black Folks"; Seems like these DAMNED

WORDS take on a life of their own and become more important than deeds to otherwise rational, intelligent people."

Suddenly Jo realized that she was sinning a whole lot; not only was she harboring anger and resentment, she was actually using swear words in her prayers. Grandma Simmons always told her that it was as much a sin to think a swear word as it was to say one and, if that was so, then she would surely go to hell unless she changed her ways. She forced herself to think of more pleasant and less sinful things.

CHAPTER 33

New Company Policy

As Jo was struggling to understand and deal with the changes happening around her, Ray was becoming increasingly alarmed about things that were happening at the mill. The company was embarking on a massive modernization and expansion project. Included in this project were plans to make the Tannerville mill the largest and best-equipped plant of its kind anywhere in the world. As the project unfolded, many new positions were being created; this, along with the emerging civil rights movement, prompted company headquarters to issue a directive that future promotional opportunities and job upgrades would be announced to all employees and awarded, to interested applicants, based on merit and company seniority. The goal of this policy was to give preferential treatment to employees, white and black, who had served the company long and well.

This policy change sparked a short period of griping by department managers who sensed some of their authority slipping away and a mild uproar by white union officials, who up to this point had such a lock on promotions that they were often able to secure the best jobs for themselves or their relatives.

In a matter of weeks, things seemed to settle down; managers appeared to be accepting the corporate directive; job-opening announcements were posted on work area bulletin boards; black and white employees began applying for the posted promotional opportunities.

Ray, now Assistant Superintendent of Finishing and Shipping, was running one of the best-trained and most productive crews in the entire company. Over the years, it had been his custom to train and develop each of his employees, without regard to race, into a top-notch worker. He had a company-wide reputation for being a fair man who provided all his employees with opportunities to excel. His crew functioned well as a team; there was very little jealousy or friction among them, just healthy competition.

Ray knew that many in his crew could easily handle the new jobs that were opening up. While he hated the thought of losing valued crewmembers, he was pleased that many of them would have a chance to move up within the company. He watched with interest as various members of his crew applied for some of the new jobs. Soon he began to notice that a disproportionate number of whites were getting jobs that he knew should have gone to better-qualified blacks from his crew.

When he questioned his crew about this, they said things like, "That's jus' the way thangs are." - "I withdrew my application 'cause I want to stay right where I am." - "My wife told me to stay workin' in your crew; she trusts you." - "I reckon that job would be too hard on me so I dropped out of the runnin'."

Ray strongly suspected that there was more going on than met the eye. He based his suspicion, in part, on the fact that his crew had always spoken with him openly and honestly; now they were vague, evasive, and uncommunicative when he attempted to learn why they were not getting any of the new jobs. He knew that most of these men had families to feed and they could darned well use the higher salaries that the new jobs paid; it just didn't seem logical that they wouldn't go after them.

During this period, Jo fell in love for the very first time. She was just in her early teens; but she deeply loved a young man four years older than she was. He happened to be named Archie and Jo saw this as an omen. She was sure she would 'live happily ever after, with her Archie, just as her Grace was doing with the man she called 'Archie'.

Unfortunately, that was not the case. Jo refused to 'go all the way' with Archie. She had been taught that it was a sin to do that until you married; in fact, she carried a load of guilt because of the heavy petting in which she and Archie indulged. When Archie failed to show up for a Saturday night date, Jo called his mother and learned that he 'had to go to Mississippi and marry Reba, because she is pregnant' Jo felt a fool. She went a bit crazy and out of control. She couldn't face her friends at school, so she wouldn't go, she hung around the downtown bus station all day, she broke curfew, and finally left home to live with a girl she met at the bus station. This girl's mother worked nights as a cocktail waitress and this gave Jo and her friend the freedom to do pretty much as they pleased. Ray hired a private detective who soon found Jo and the court sent het to the State Training School in East Lake until she was 18 years old.

Ray's pensive mood had not escaped Grace's notice, and one evening as they sat over after-supper coffee, she questioned him about it. "Archie, I know you well and I see that you're mullin' somethin' over in your mind; you've been doin' it for a few weeks. Don't you think it's time to tell me about it?"

"I guess you're right; it has to be dealt with sooner or later and I reckon sooner is best."

"This isn't a small thing is it?"

"No, it's not. Shorty, the niggers at the mill aren't gettin' a fair shot at the new jobs. Some of my crew deserve those jobs and should be gettin' them; but they're not. Hell, you've seen and talked with most of 'em enough to know how smart and dedicated the fellows in my crew are."

"They're a good bunch alright. How can this happen, Archie? I mean the new policy that ya'll got from headquarters pretty much says the new jobs have to go to the best workers."

"Aw hell, when some of them ole boys down at the mill take it in their head to resist somethin', they can be real good at goin' through the motions and makin' it look like they're following orders while they doin' as they damned well please. I just didn't think they'd try it with somethin' that's this important to the company and I haven't yet figured out how they are gettin' the niggers to go along with 'em."

"I guess when you figure it out you'll try to fix it, won't you?"

"I don't want to open this nasty can of worms but I don't see how I can get out of it. I feel in my bones that this situation is apt to get real mean before we're done with it. The first thing I've got to do is get you and Cary out of harm's way as best I can. I'm not too concerned about the girls; Margaret Ann's apartment is all the way on the far side of Le Grande; and; our "little black sheep" is shaping up nicely in East Lake. I don't think either of them will be much affected by anything happenin' at the mill".

"You know Archie I never thought I would think this, much less say it; but, maybe, bein' away from us is the wake-up call Jo needs to get her life back on track.

"I think you're right, she seems to be doin' fine up there."

Continuing to sip his coffee and mull over the situation, Ray mused; "I think maybe we should move on over to that property that we bought in Parkville. We may have to put up with some primitive livin' arrangements until I can get us a proper house built over there but we'll manage. I don't like having you live around a bunch of mill workers now that things are becoming so volatile, and I worry about Cary being in the Quarters so much. It's not the niggers that I'm worried about; they wouldn't harm any of us, and besides most of them are so used to Cary bein' over there that half the time they forget that he isn't black. I worry that some hotheaded, white, mill workers may take a notion to harm you or him as a way to get me to back off. So what do you say; are you Ok with movin' over to Parkville?"

"I'd love to; I like livin' where I'm able to walk down to the bay or the creek and fish any time I take a notion to. I know Cary will be happy; every time we spend a weekend campin' over there, he hates to leave. I just wish the move wasn't bein' driven by a mess at the mill and I wish there was some way you could stay out of it."

"So do I, Shorty, so do I."

An increasing number of black workers began showing up for work with injuries inflicted by physical violence. This alarmed Ray, but he instinctively understood that it would be useless to try questioning any of his crew while they were at the mill; so, he devised means to talk with them on their own turf. At the end of the shift, he stayed at his desk looking over paper work, would call out a brief, distracted sounding "good Evenin'" to his crewmembers as they left. When he sure one or two of his workers were off mill property and walking home, he would get in his car, 'just happen' to be driving in the direction of the Quarters, and offer them a lift. Other times, he would 'just happen' to run out of cigarettes when he was near the grocery store in the Quarters and pop in to buy a pack. He used these, so-called, chance encounters to inquire discreetly about what was going on. Away from the mill, his crew-members spoke freely to him because they trusted him and knew that he cared about their welfare; they told him how the local labor unions were sending out goon squads to 'discourage' blacks from applying for the new jobs.

It was more or less an open secret that white bigots largely controlled the union. What Ray, and very few others at the mill, knew was that many of these union men, along with some of the top managers at the local mill, were Klansmen. Some of these Klansmen knew that Ray's father had been active in the Klan prior to his death. They assumed, incorrectly, that Ray shared his father's racist views and didn't guard their tongues around him as carefully as they did around other managers and supervisors at the mill.

Ray felt very strongly that this problem must be dealt with; furthermore, he knew that trying to get it dealt with on a local level could very well blow up in his face. He became frustrated by the compulsion to take some action; yet, he wasn't sure what the action should be. He contented himself with keeping his eyes and ears open, discretely collecting any information and documentation he could get his hands on, being careful not to alert anyone at the local mill that he was doing this, and biding his time until he figure out what the best course of action was.

CHAPTER 34

Ray Goes to New York

Grace was scheduled for surgery to correct a 'female problem' that had plagued her for over a year; Ray had arranged his schedule so that he could be with her during her hospital stay; then, he got word he was needed in New York immediately.

His milk carton design was considered a real breakthrough product; company directors were convinced that it would generate a great deal of revenue. They had filed for a patent and needed Ray in New York to consult with company officials and engineers regarding the specifications for the machinery that would be required to mass-produce this revolutionary product.

Even though he was delighted that his latest invention had been so well received by the industry, Ray didn't want to make a trip to New York at this time; he felt that his place was with Grace. She, on the other hand, insisted that she was not a 'fragile Southern Belle', and would be fine on her own.

In spite of her assurances, Ray spoke to his bosses in New York about putting off this trip. The start of the project was dependant on consulting with Ray; hence, they would grant no delay. However, the bosses were willing to rearrange meetings and allow him to be home on the day of Grace's surgery and remain with her for a couple of days before returning to New York.

With these arrangements confirmed, Ray talked with Margaret Ann; "Honey, I'm between a rock and a hard place and I really need you to help me out. I can't put off my trip to New York, and the best deal I could get out of those boys at headquarters was to let me fly home the day of Grace's surgery; however, my flight won't leave until after her surgery has begun. Can you get a day off and be at the hospital with Grace until I can get there? The surgery seems pretty straight forward and there shouldn't be any complication - but, I'm gonna' have you listed as the person to make decisions in my absence, OK?"

Margaret Ann was flattered that her Daddy trusted her to handle such a grown up situation. Her response sounded more confident than she actually felt. "Of course, I can do it, Daddy. I've got vacation time available, and taking a day off won't be a problem."

At eighteen, Margaret Ann's experience with doctors had been very limited, and she hadn't been inside a hospital since she had her appendix removed at age five. She was scared to death about taking on this responsibility but tried to hide her fear from her Daddy.

On the appointed day, Margaret Ann took the day off from work, escorted Grace to the hospital, helped her check in, and paced the waiting room floor during the surgery. After what seemed like forever; Grace's doctor came into the waiting room and approached Margaret Ann. "The surgery went very well and there are no complications. You look a little pale, why don't you go down to the cafeteria and get some coffee or iced tea? It'll be about an hour before Grace is out of recovery and you can see her."

Now that she had spoken with the doctor, Margaret Ann relaxed a bit and was able to enjoy a cup of coffee; after that, she browsed in the gift shop and bought a bouquet of flowers for Grace. When she arrived in Grace's room, she was shocked; Grace was all pale, groggy, and hooked up to an IV. The relaxed feeling evaporated, and she was again terrified that something would go wrong.

Margaret Ann had been sitting beside Grace's bed for about two hours, when the door opened; she looked up expecting to see one of the nurses, instead, there was her Daddy. His eyes were red rimmed, his shirt collar was unbuttoned, his tie was hanging loosely around his neck, and his business suit was all rumpled; nonetheless, he looked wonderful to Margaret Ann. She had never been happier to see him.

Ray saw the look of joy in Margaret Ann's eyes and the relief that registered on her face; he opened his arms, and enveloped her in a bear hug. "It's OK now, honey. I figured that you would be a little scared, but I was sure that I could count on you; I just talked to the doctor and he said you did just fine."

With a sigh of relief, Margaret Ann leaned her head on her Daddy's shoulder and thought, "Nothing bad can happen now 'cause Daddy's here to take care of everything."

Shortly after Ray returned to New York, Warren, a company executive that he knew and trusted, invited him to dinner. Over after-dinner drinks, Ray approached the subject of problems at the Tannerville mill with his host.

"Warren, you and I have known each other a long time and you know that I'm not a hot-head or a trouble maker; some of what I'm about to tell you will be hard to believe and you may not want to hear it; if that's the case you just stop me, OK?"

"Ray, to the best of my knowledge, we've always been open and above board with each other. I see no reason not to believe anything you tell me and, of course, I want to hear what you have to say."

Encouraged; Ray began, "What's goin' on down at the Tannerville mill is totally out of line with company policy; some of it's criminal and in the long run it's goin' to reflect very badly on the company if nothing's done to stop it."

"I've heard a few rumors and tried to check them out; but so far, I haven't been able to nail anything down. Ray, I don't for one minute doubt the integrity of your information and I very much want to hear what you have to say; but before you proceed, I want to be sure that you're aware that I'll feel compelled to act on the information once you share it with me. You do understand that; don't you?"

"Yes, I understand and I was hopin' you'd feel that way."

Ray told Warren what he knew of the happenings at the Tannerville mill, provided as much detail and documentation as he could, and when he finished, Warren was aghast.

"Wow, this is potentially an explosive situation and it looks like you're square in the middle of it. The company just isn't going to ignore or tolerate racial bigotry. Naturally, I have to inform the board about this and I'm hoping that you'll help me with the presentation; will you?"

"I'm in this thing pretty deep and don't know of any way out except to help y'all correct the situation; so, yes, of course, I'll help you."

"I'll try to shield you from as much of the fall out as I can; however, you'll be in for some rough times once word of this gets on the company grapevine, and you know that it will."

"Aw Hell, Warren, I'm miles ahead of you - not all southerners are slow." Ray joked.

Warren was glad that Ray had lightened the mood a little. "OK, Mister Greased Lightning, lets get down to brass tacks about what is going on and how to approach this thing with the board members."

When Warren and Ray made their presentation to the board, it voted unanimously to get the situation cleaned up no matter what it took. The boards' remedy was to put together a team of undercover investigators and send them to Tannerville; the mission of this team was to verify and expand the information Ray had gathered.

The board didn't want Ray anywhere near the local mill while the investigation was underway; nor did they want him seen around town talking with any of the investigative team or doing anything out of the ordinary. They realized that Ray had gone way out on a limb to assist them and they intended to do everything in their power to protect this valuable employee and his family.

The plan was to have Ray go back to Tannerville long enough to prepare one or two of his most trusted crewmembers for the undercover teams impending arrival. Then, he would leave for, what the company would describe as, an inspection tour of the southern mills in conjunction with the pending installation of new machinery required to mass-produce his new milk carton.

The reality was that, in addition to protecting Ray while the investigators were at the mill, he was to seek out any evidence that union bosses and/or local management at the mills he visited were trying to circumvent the hiring and promotion of blacks.

For the next two and a half months, Ray traveled to mills in Florida, Georgia, Mississippi, Arkansas and North Carolina, and when the investigative team needed his input, they arranged to get it via phone or arrange an out of town meeting, well away from Tannerville.

Ray revealed the true nature of his travels to Grace, but Cary was shielded from this information.

As the extent of the corruption and civil rights abuses at the paper mill were uncovered, it became apparent that this situation was much too dangerous and complex to be dealt with internally. The FBI was brought in to take over the investigation, oversee the protection of those employees who had helped with the investigation, and to build cases against those whose crimes were punishable by law.

During his first briefing by the FBI, Ray requested that his role in this be kept as quiet as possible and that his family be provided protection. Company executives and the FBI assured Ray that the entire house-cleaning operation was being conducted in a very low-key manner and that the FBI had already assigned agents to protect each member of his family. They explained to Ray that these agents would be like 'guardian angels', undetected and unobtrusive but close by and capable of protecting and assisting any family member, if needed.

The FBI met with the local media and requested that they keep details of this operation out of the public eye as much as possible. The media cooperated and printed very little about the scope of the civil wrongs or about the action taken to correct them, and they printed virtually nothing regarding Ray's pivotal role.

Cary was now high school; he was proficient on the drums, baritone sax and clarinet, very involved in the school's music department, and a respected member of the band. He knew the physical layout of the music department like the back of his hand; so, when a new music teacher joined the department, it seemed natural that Cary be asked to help him learn the ropes. Cary had not a clue that this man was actually an FBI 'angel' whose current job was to ensure that no harm came to him.

Like many teenagers, Cary spent little time thinking about integration and most assuredly didn't suspect that his father was directly involved in it.

CHAPTER 35

Settlin' in Parkville

The Simmons's property in Parkville was a bit over an acre in size and had over 200 standing trees, lots of thick underbrush and climbing vines. Many of the Simmons's neighbors had opted to clear their land by simply bulldozing it and planting new young trees where they wanted them. Ray didn't see the logic of dozing big beautiful trees then waiting years for newly planted ones to become mature enough to provide any shade. Instead, he and Cary, using an old-fashioned crosscut saw, felled all the standing dead trees and the few live ones that would interfere with construction. Beyond felling the trees, most of the land clearing was accomplished by Grace and Cary because Ray was traveling so much the summer that they moved to Parkville.

Cary, like his parents, was a confirmed coffee drinker. Most afternoons he and Grace would fortify themselves with two or three cups of coffee, pick up their machetes, pruning shears, and maddoxes, and spend a couple of hours clearing underbrush or digging up roots of dead trees from the area that would eventually become their yard. Grace was small in statue but she could swing a grubbin' hoe with the best of 'em.

Whenever Ray could schedule a break in his travels, He would spend a few days at home helping Grace and Cary. During one of these breaks, he mounted a large spotlight high up on a sweet gum tree at the edge of a large clearing that Cary and Grace had created. After that, it was possible to work well into the night, continuing to clear more of the land.

By the end of the summer, Ray had built a tool shed, sunk a well, built a pump-house, and installed an electric jet pump in it. Cary was very grateful for this well because it relieved him of the daily chore of carting water from a neighbor's home, several hundred yards away. Ray bought a 14' camp trailer for them to live in. The trailer was set up on the left side of the pump house and tool shed. Ray, Cary and Grace spent many happy hours at the trailer's small kitchen table drinking coffee, planning how to landscape the yard, discussing Cary's high school activities, and endlessly arguing fishin' strategy.

To the right of the pump house and tool shed, Ray built a frame, consisting of a wood floor, walls two feet high, and about five feet above the walls, he built a 2 by 2 rafter. He slipped a 7'x7' tent, purchased from an Army surplus store, over this rafter, anchored it to the walls, equipped it with a screen door and dubbed it 'Cary's room'.

Cary loved living in his tent house; it was furnished with a captain's bunk that Ray salvaged from an old decommissioned Navy ship, a small chest of drawers, a desk and chair, an overhead light, a reading lamp, an electric heater, and a shortwave radio that Cary had assembled as a science project a year earlier. The tool shed and pump house were positioned between the trailer, where Ray and Grace slept and Cary's tent. This afforded him plenty of privacy; he could slip out to D' Olive Creek, spend most of the night froggin', walk home just before dawn, put his catch in a refrigerator in the tool shed, and slip into bed without his parents knowing he had been out. When it was too cold or rainy to go froggin', Cary would stay in and spend hours tuning his shortwave in to far away, exotic locations and dream of visiting them someday.

Most afternoons, twilight would find Cary and Grace on the shore of the bay or at the mouth of D' Olive Creek, with a thermos of coffee between them, trying to catch the 'big one'.

One afternoon as Grace was wading in the shallows and bait-casting into the bay, she spotted what appeared to be a large log floating not far off. She noticed it because it appeared to be floating against the current and not with it. As it grew nearer, she realized it was an alligator and it must be close to 12' long. She called out Cary, who was nearby, and pointed it out to him. "Look, over yonder, you ever see that guy around here before?" she asked.

"No, I'm sure would remember if I had seem him before; he must be the granddaddy of them all!"

As Grace and Cary were discussing the 'gator, Mr. Hill, a neighbor who owned a summer home nearby, came along; Mr. Hill was a nice guy, but he was a 'city-slicker' who didn't often wander down to the bay shore this late in the afternoon, and had never seen a 'gator there before. When he spotted the 'gator he exclaimed, "My God! Y'all better come on out of the water, I'll go get my shotgun."

Grace exclaimed, "Whatever for? Shotgun pellets would just bounce off his hide, and besides, he's not harmin' anybody."

"But isn't he dangerous?"

"Not really", but if he's bothering you I'll shoo 'em away." She grabbed a piece of driftwood, walked over to the 'gator, and whacked him a couple of times on his back. The 'gator turned and looked at her, then swam docilely away while Cary and Mr. Hill stared in amazement.

When Ray was not traveling, it wasn't unusual for him and Cary to spend a whole afternoon listening to their record collection, which was extensive and included all styles of music; classical, pop, jazz, rhythm & blues, bluegrass, country, and even the emerging style called rock & roll and rockabilly music. If they were especially moved or inspired by a specific passage of music, they played it repeatedly while dissecting what the artist did or didn't do that made that specific passage great.

"Cary, how about puttin' on that old record that Vera and Sam gave us; you know, the one of Mississippi John Hurt. I'm in the mood for some good blues."

Cary found the requested record, put it on the turntable, and Ray sighed, "Listen to this ole boy. I'll tell you that nigger can stand up on a stage with nothing but the voice God gave him and his cheap knock box guitar and put on a show that's really something. I saw him once over in Hattiesburg and he had the audience eating out of the palm of his hand."

"Yes, he sure is a good blues man."

"You know son, music is as much craft as it is art. If you don't work at it, I don't care how much raw talent you have, you just won't be consistently good. Ole John Hurt understands this, and that's why he is so good. He's got real talent, but he's not too lazy to work at it some."

"I don't know Daddy, seems that amplifiers and some of the more modern sound systems help quite a bit; don't you think?"

"They help a good performer sound some better, they can't mask lack of talent or a shoddy performance."

"I reckon you're right.   Sometimes when I haven't been practicing much or I'm a little off my feed and not playin' so good during band practice, that darn new sound system in the band room just makes it worse."

CHAPTER 36

Snake Spit

Ray arrived home from the mill one Friday evening, discovered Grace and Cary still clearing land, realized how hard they had been working, and decided to reward all their hard work. "Hey, you two, take a break and come sit in the shade; I want to talk with ya'll."

"What's up?" Cary was glad to lay down his grubbin' hoe and relax for a bit.

"Yeah, Archie; what's up?" Grace echoed.

"Remember how ole Earl Moore was always braggin' about the good fishin' along the Pearl River?"

Grace and Cary nodded their heads.

"I think it's time we see if he knows what he's talkin' about, don't y'all?"

"Sounds fine to me." Cary stood, picked up his grubbin' hoe, and started walking back to the area he and Grace had been clearing. "You gonna get up a trip for after we're done with this land clearin'?"

"Nope; we're gonna go right now, that is unless y'all would rather stay here and clear more land. I'm figurin' to go on over to Mississippi this afternoon, camp on the beach, get up early, and get in a few hours of fishin' before headin' home tomorrow."

"That's the best offer I've had in a long time." Grace called over her shoulder; she was already heading for the trailer to round up the ice chest, her fishin' gear, and their camping supplies.

Cary dropped the grubbin' hoe and yelled, "Count me in" as he headed for his tent to get his fishin' gear and a change of clothes.

In less than an hour, the car was loaded and they were heading out - North to Spanish Fort - across the Causeway - through Bankhead Tunnel - out Government Street (US 90) and through Mobile. In Theodore, Ray stopped at Foster's Gas Station to fill the tank; tank full they continued through Grand Bay and on into

Mississippi - Pascagoula - Ocean Springs; - Biloxi. Grace loved the stretch of Highway 90 that ran from Point Cadet in Biloxi, into Bay St. Louis. Called Beach Boulevard, this was one of the most scenic routes along the Gulf Coast; on one side of Beach Boulevard was Mississippi Sound, miles of beaches, with sand so fine that she called them "sugar sand" beaches, and a charming old Lighthouse. On the other side, huge antebellum homes with beautiful shady lawns, magnolia trees dripping Spanish moss, Beauvior - the Jefferson Davis Shrine - and Gus Stevens Seafood House.

The Seafood house served a "Whop Salad" that Grace really enjoyed, so Ray stopped there for supper. The menu offered Whop Salad in two sizes - big or small. Grace had worked up a huge appetite clearing land; she wondered if she should order a "big Whop". In the past, she had always ordered the small one and it was almost more than she could eat. As she was trying to make up her mind, a waiter neared the table carrying the biggest bowl of salad she had ever seen. "Excuse me", she to the waiter, "what is that dish?"

"It's a big Whop", Ma'am." came the reply. That made the decision for Grace; she was sticking to a small one.

After supper, the Simmons continued their journey, through Gulfport, Long Beach, Pas Christian, Bay St. Louis, and Waveland. They reached the Pearl River around mid-night, found a nice spot to camp, and grabbed a few hours of sleep.

Next morning, not long after day light, they saw a beautiful wide, winding body of water; lined with many secluded coves and shady beaches that gave easy assess to nice fishin' holes. Ray selected a cove that appeared to house a likely fishin' hole; his selection proved to be right on the money, and fishing in Pearl River proved to be as good as Earl claimed. By late morning, each of them had caught their limit.

On the drive home, Ray grew a little weary and began looking for a place to stop and stretch his legs. He spotted a grassy area with a couple of picnic tables out in front of an old, unpainted building; a sign next to the building proclaimed, "Brand New - Just Opened - REPTILE JUNGLE - Stop In and See Us."

Ray chose to stop here; he figured that in addition to getting a little exercise and rest from driving, he would take Grace and Cary through the 'Reptile Jungle' and teach Cary a little more about snakes.

The Reptile Jungle had long winding hallways, lined along one side with snake cages. Actually, they were homemade chicken coop type of enclosures and they housed snakes from many different countries as well as different areas of the USA.

A friendly teenaged boy, probably the son or nephew of the owner, was tending the place. He clearly liked snakes and wanted to please his customers. Grace, unlike most female customers that the teenager had seen, showed a genuine interest in snakes; she and the boy straightaway struck up a rapport; he happily answered her questions and rattled off what he knew about each particular type of snake as they wandered from cage to cage.

When they came to a cage that contained three adult king cobras, the teenager informed Grace, "We got these directly from India, just a few weeks ago."

The cobras were just lying in their cage, with their hoods relaxed, not moving much. Grace commented, with a note of disappointment in her voice, "It's a shame that we can't see their hoods. I've seen pictures of cobras with open hoods and they're very impressive."

The eager teenager, wanting to please his new buddy, picked up a straightened-out coat hanger and began poking the snakes to make them rise up and open their hood. As one of them rose and began to spread open its hood, Cary became intrigued and began to move closer to the cage to get a better look.

At that moment, Ray, who had been walking a little behind them, came at a dead run; and with a sudden swing of his arm, he knocked Cary backwards. Cary landed on the floor a good three or four feet from the cage and began to cry, both from the physical pain caused when Ray's arm hit him and from the shock and embarrassment of being struck so unexpended by his gentle Daddy.

Grace rushed to Cary's side to comfort him, glared at Ray, and hissed, "Have you lost your mind?"

Ray reached around Grace, gently picked Cary up and began to explain his action. "Cary, the instant you moved toward that cobra, it began zeroing in on you and aiming poisonous venom at your eyes."

Ray pointed to a fresh wet spot on the wall at exactly the height where Cary's head would have been had Ray not knocked him out of the way; he continued his explanation. "The cobra spits venom into the eyes of its prey or attackers in order to blind them so that they are unable to run away before it can sink in its fangs. That cobra targeted you because, by suddenly moving toward it, you appeared to be attacking."

Seeing his son in danger from a snake for the second time reminded Ray how fragile life can be and the thought of losing his son brought a lump to his throat. He checked Cary over very carefully to make sure there was no splash of venom on him and walked with his arm around Cary's shoulder for the remainder of their visit to the Reptile Jungle.

Before they left, Ray talked with the teenager; carefully explaining how the cobra could spit venom a good many feet. He wanted to be sure that the boy understood that he was not angry and had no intention of causing trouble over an incident in which no actual harm had been done. However, he did suggest, strongly, that the boy ask his boss to install a Plexiglas shield in front of the cobra cage for the protection of future customers. The boy assured Ray that he would do that and thanked him for taking time to explain the habits of the cobra.

A few weeks after that incident, Grace called the Reptile Jungle to see if they had indeed put a shield in front of the cobra cage. The same teenager who had been there during their visit answered the phone and she greeted him warmly and asked; "Did you get your boss to put up a shield in front of the cobra cage?"

His cheery reply came right away; "Yes ma'am, he sure did. It was put up the next day. By the way, I've got a new job now."

Alarmed, Grace exclaimed, "You mean you got fired for suggesting the shield?"

"No, no, nothin' like that." the boy cried; "Anytime we have visitors, I'm allowed to prod the snakes a little and get them to display those magnificent hoods. Now, anytime the snakes decide to spit at somebody, it's my job to wash the snake-spit off the screen, but I don't mind at all as long as I can show folks those hoods!"

At supper that evening, Grace shared the story with Ray and Cary; the three of them had a good chuckle over the young fellow being so excited about cleaning snake-spit.

CHAPTER 37

Integration Comes to the University

Jo had developed into a mature, intelligent, and trustworthy teen; so, she was allowed to attend the public high school in town and return to the State facility at night. She was a senior when a young black woman attempted to integrate the University of Alabama, in Tuscaloosa. The principal and teachers at Jo's high school felt that this was an important historic event; hence, they arranged for television sets to be placed in classrooms so that students could witness it.

Sitting in her classroom, Jo saw Alabama State Troopers holding back mobs of angry white people who had gathered along the road leading to the University and around the University steps. She watched with intense interest as the camera panned to a big, black, sedan that slowly moved along the road and stopped in front of the University steps. When the car stopped, the mob pushed in as close to the car as the troopers would allow; they began waving Confederate flags, shaking their fists, and shouting obscenities at the car.

A young black woman, looking very small and scared, got out of the car and began walking up the University steps; as she proceeded, the mob began to chant, "Nigger! Nigger! You better go back - cause if you don't your head you'll lack". Many of the students in Jo's classroom began chanting along with the crowd on TV.

Jo looked around the classroom, expecting to see teachers disapproving of the students' action; instead she saw them grinning and nudging each other as though they approved of this conduct.

This incident aroused conflicting emotions in Jo; she felt fear for the black girl who faced the hostile mob with such dignity; she felt excited and a little caught up in the festive mood of her fellow students and the mob on TV. She also felt self-disgust, because she seemed unable to abide by the teachings of her parents - "don't buy into the 'bully mentality' of any mob; think situations through for yourself and act accordingly." She was physically sick to her stomach and having a hard time sorting out her emotions. She was ashamed of being too intimidated to voice her objections, and she kept thinking "There stands a black girl, not much older than me, facing a mass of reporters and a very hostile crowd and here I sit afraid to chance pissing off a few of my classmates by objecting to their conduct." At that moment, she felt like the world's biggest hypocrite and coward.

Within a week of being admitted to the University, the young black girl was expelled; University officials said that her presence caused excessive unrest and tension on campus, and this atmosphere was making it impossible for anyone to learn. Furthermore, they proclaimed, that this situation could not be allowed to continue, so she had to go.

The NAACP loudly protested this action and vowed there would be much trouble for the state of Alabama over this matter.

Jo could not shake her feeling that somehow this whole situation, from beginning to end, just was not right. To her way of thinking, attempting to become the first black student at an all white University, in the Deep South didn't seem like a natural act for someone as naïve, shy and frightened, as this girl appeared to be. Every time this girl's picture appeared on TV or in the papers she had a 'deer caught in headlights' look and seemed to want to be anywhere but where she was.

Jo needed to talk about this situation; she no longer trusted any of her teachers to understand or care what she was experiencing; she felt that her peers at school would be of no help in sorting out her emotions; so, as she usually did, she called home and talked it over with her Daddy.

"Daddy, I keep thinking about this situation at the University of Alabama."

"Why's that, Cricket?"

"It sorta' seems like that girl really doesn't want to be doin' this; she always looks like she's about to cry. Daddy, she must have known that tryin' to integrate the University of Alabama would cause all kinds of trouble and put her in the middle of it."

"Yes, I imagine she knew that."

"Well, then why'd she do it? It's obvious that she don't know how to stand up to bullies. I mean, if she just wants a good education there's Tuskegee or lots of other Negro colleges that she can go to. It's kinda like she was forced into this."

"Sometimes, Jo, you're wise beyond your years. I can't imagine that she decided on her own; I suspect that somebody - or a bunch of somebodies - pushed her pretty hard; it could've been her folks, but most likely, it was the NAACP or some well-meaning whites that pushed her into doing it. I just hope that whoever got her into this mess hasn't caused her to ruin her life."

"Daddy, can't folks see that things are startin' to change down here; if they would just slow down, maybe things would sort themselves out. Why do they have to push so hard to have everything happen at once?"

"The NAACP is trying to get a toe hold in down here and they need a cause to draw attention to themselves. Plus, there are lots of white people who strongly believe that niggers deserve equality and they're really trying to help. Unfortunately, some of them are convinced that the only way to accomplish anything is to get up in everybody's face, make them admit that they've been wrong all these years, and force them to make drastic changes right away. This attitude causes the kind of things that we just witnessed at the University. Anytime you get up in the face of a stubborn red neck and try to force him to admit he was wrong, he'll fight you every way he can, even when he knows that you have a valid point."

"They sure made a mess of this, didn't they? The University still isn't integrated and with the TV and newspapers going on about what she did, that girl will have a hard time fitting in anywhere she tries to go to school."

"You just concentrate on what you need to do to graduate and let this situation sort its self out."

"OK, Daddy, thanks; talkin' to you always helps."

Jo did as her Daddy advised and, having lost respect for many of her teachers and classmates, she was glad to graduate and leave Birmingham in June.

The following September, she married her high school sweetheart, who was now in the Air Force, and began life as a military wife. As she became involved in her new live, thought of integration receded to the back of her mind.

CHAPTER 38

Klan Threats

Unfortunately, in spite of all the efforts of the paper company executives and the FBI, the white supremacist grapevine began circulating information that Ray Simmons, "that rotten nigger loving traitor", was co-operating with those "damn yankees who are investigating the mill". Some folks claimed that he was responsible for the downfall of many of the "staunch defenders of the supreme white race".

The FBI moved quickly and effectively to shield Ray's family from harm; they did their job so well that the only lifestyle change that directly affected Cary was his use of the family phone.

Grace had little use for phones, relying on them only when she felt it necessary to relay or receive some important information in a timely manner. She considered talking on the phone for hours, as some of her friends and family did, to be just plain silly; and, in her opinion, it was second only to watching soap operas as the world's biggest waste of time.

Ray was practically phone-phobic; when he got a call about a problem at the mill, even in the middle of the night or on his days off, he would usually drive to the mill to deal with matters face to face rather than talk with what he referred to as 'disembodied voices'.

Cary, like most children of the 50's, saw the phone as a cool thing and while he didn't talk excessively on the phone, he was the major telephone user in the household and most of the incoming calls were for him.

One day, seemingly out of the blue, Ray abruptly informed Cary, "From now on you are not to answer the phone under any circumstances; I'll be the only one to answer it and when I'm not home it'll just go unanswered. Is that clear?"

Bewilderingly, Cary queried, "Yes sir, but why? Is there a problem with how much I'm on the phone?"

"You've done nothin' wrong but my new rule isn't open for discussion; that's just how I want it for now," snapped Ray.

It was unlike Ray to speak in such a snappish tone of voice or to, so curtly, refuse to explain a seemingly arbitrary and illogical rule. This behavior struck Cary as odd in the extreme; however, he just shrugged it off as strange adult quirk and with his recently acquired know-it-all teenaged attitude, he attributed to yet another example of aged wisdom clipping the wings of youth.

Cary was mildly curious about the increase in the number of calls that his Daddy said were "wrong number" or "just somebody for me". However, given his Daddy's bizarre new attitude about the phone, he never mentioned it and surely never suspected that these calls were actually hate calls and death threats from the Klan or other white supremacists. He had no way of knowing that the new phone rule was just one of many ways his Daddy tried to shield him from these vicious people and their hateful, bigoted beliefs.

Cary wished that he could talk with his sister, Jo, about their Daddy's strange phone rules and Grace's recent unexplained dictate that he stay close to home when not in school. However, Jo was now married and living near Robbins Air Force base in Georgia; so, Cary's opportunities to see or talk with her were few and far between.

Jo saw nothing amiss when a Georgia Highway Patrolman and his wife moved into a house across the street from the one she had recently rented, in a neighborhood where mostly military personnel lived; furthermore, it seemed natural that the two families, both new to the area, would rapidly become friends. If anyone had suggested to her that this couple were undercover FBI agents assigned to protect her family, Jo would have laughed at the notion.

Since Jo's marriage, she was kept so busy tending her growing family and relocating from one place to another when her husband's duty station changed, that she had little time to ponder the question of integration or the growing Civil Rights Movement. Recently her attention focused on these things because of the TV coverage of the governor of Alabama. Seeing her old friend Beau Williams standing in the doorway of the University of Alabama attempting to stop two black students from entering that school was a bitter reminder of the earlier attempt to integrate the University and the turmoil that had caused.

Jo's childhood encounter with Williams had impressed her, and she continued to have a warm spot in her heart for him; she admired him, and was pleased when he won the race for Governor of Alabama. Now, it frustrated her to see her Beau Williams on the University steps, looking very impressive, doing what he said was his duty and "what the folks who elected me expect me to do". She couldn't deny a thrill of admiration and pride when she saw his face. After all how many folks could claim that a friend from their childhood was now governor of their home state.

Williams appeared so very sincere in his belief that he was doing the right thing; however, Jo felt that he was misguided and that this wasn't the right thing to do. She wasn't sure just what the right thing was, but she felt a sense of disappointment that the Governor couldn't find a better way to handle the situation.

She didn't dwell on these thoughts for long; her husband was on a TDY assignment to a radar site in the Nevada desert and she was busy managing her children and household; she was totally unprepared for what happened less than a week after she saw Beau Williamson on TV.

Early one afternoon, Jo heard a car pull into her driveway and the sound of someone walking on her porch; when she opened her front door, she saw a young Air Force officer and the base Chaplin, her knees went weak and she whispered, "Has something happened to my husband?"

"No! No! No!" The Chaplin rushed forward while rapidly assuring her, "Nothing's wrong with your husband, Mrs. Monroe. May we come in for a few minutes?"

Jo mutely pushed the screen door open and allowed them entry. She quickly sat down because she felt lightheaded and, in spite of the denial, she was still shaken and afraid that something was amiss with her husband.

"Mrs. Monroe, um… we know that your husband is on TDY and… uh… that you have two small children." The young officer spoke in an unsure and rather hesitant manner. "We… er… that is… the… er… the Air Force would like for you to stay on the base temporarily… uh… just, in case... um … that is, you may need some help with the children while your husband is gone."

"Y'all think I'm stupid or what?" Jo demanded; she was now more angry than scared. "The first time my husband was on TDY, my allotment check got lost in the mail, which left me with no money and nobody at the base would help me straightenin' that out; I actually had to borrow food from neighbors. The last time he was TDY, my baby got infected ears and y'all wouldn't even notify him that his child was sick - fed me some BS about not wantin' him distracted by home problems. I could've used a little physical help from y'all. Trying to juggle carin' for my son, makin' sure the baby got her medicine, and getting' back and forth to the base clinic so often was a real nightmare. But, guess what! When I called the base to see if I could get any help and I couldn't get anybody, includin' you," she emphasized, pointing to

the Chaplin, "to talk to me on the phone or return my calls. "
Now, out of the blue, when I'm doin' just fine, you come to my
house and invite me to stay on the base. Well, I'm not stupid', so
ya'll might as well march right out of here or tell me what's really
going on."

The young officer asked in a brisk tone of voice; "You're Ray
Simmons's daughter, aren't you?"

"Yes I am; and damned proud of it; is that a problem for
you?"

The young officer was not used to having anyone, especially a
military dependant, speak to him in such loud, demanding tones;
consequently, he became nervous, and began to stammer. "Yes…
er…No…, um… uh… it's just that there have… er… been some
threats made at the paper mill."

At this point Jo's neighbor burst through her door and flashed
what Jo assumed was his Highway Patrol badge; he addressed the
officer and the Chaplin in a clipped tone, "I need a private word
with the two of you out on the porch; right now."   Surprisingly,

they got up, followed him out to the porch, and left Jo sitting dumbfounded on her couch.

Once out of the house, Jo's neighbor quickly explained that they were putting his FBI cover in danger, and that he was taking control of the situation. He explained that they were the victims of a communication failure and he would straighten out the matter.

The mix-up began when a memo regarding a threat to a military dependant was sent to the base commander. The first problem was, the memo should have been clearly stamped 'INFORMATION ONLY - TAKE NO ACTION' and it was not; the second problem was, the memo should never have been routed to the base commander's office; it should have been routed directly to the Security Office. The third, and biggest, mistake was, the commander should have checked with his superiors before sending anyone to Mrs. Monroe's home, and, of course, he hadn't done so.

Jo could hear their voices on the porch but couldn't make out the conversation. Just as she was collecting her wits enough to go out and see what all this strange behavior was about, the three of them came back into the house.

Her neighbor grinned sheepishly and explained. "Well, Jo you've just experienced your first and, I hope your last, major government fowl up. Somebody over-reacted to a threat made against your Daddy by a few hotheaded mill workers. Seems, he went a little too far in trying to help some of his black workers get promotions and ticked off a few union boys. I'm sure he'll explain it when you call him."

Jo shook her head, "This is unreal, why is the Air Force even into this and how come you know more than they do?"

"No offence, fellows", her neighbor smiled at the Chaplin and the officer, "but I got worried when I saw the military car over here. I called my dispatcher to see if they knew what was going on; my dispatcher asked me to come over here and clear things up. The Highway Patrol had a request, from the base commander, to head off his boys before they reached your home; seems he had overreacted to a routine memo and was very embarrassed by this mistake. Obviously, the request came a little late."

The Chaplin apologized, "Mrs. Monroe, we're very sorry to have disturbed you. I hope you understand that we were acting in your best interest. It just so happens that our action wasn't needed." The red-faced young officer and the Chaplin quickly said their good byes and left.

Jo, still rattled by the whole affair, thanked her neighbor and rushed him out so that she could call her Daddy.

"Daddy", Jo began in a trembling tone, "It's Jo and you aren't gonna believe…"

Ray interrupted, " It's OK, Cricket, I already know all about it, now calm down or you'll scare the kids."

"But, Daddy," Jo sighed in relief, "They said…"

"I reckon I know pretty much what they said. Just forget them, OK?"

"I can't - I'm scared."

"Now listen here, young lady, you're a mother and a military wife and I expect you to behave like one. So, pay attention to me and do as you're told." Ray spoke in the firm 'no nonsense voice' that he sometimes used when Jo was a child; it had the desired effect; Jo calmed down and listened.

"Honey, it's nothin' for you to worry over, you know that I abhor bullies and there's more than a few of them at the mill. They just can't accept that the niggers are gonna get some of the good new positions, and it's about time, too. So I had to remind 'em and I wasn't real polite about it. Anyhow, it got 'em a little riled up and they behaved like bullies always do; they threatened to gang up on me and 'put me in my place'. As to how the Air Force got wind of this - God only knows, but they sure moved fast; let's hope they move that fast when they're really needed."

"Daddy, are you sure that ya'll are alright over there?" Jo wanted to know.

"Yep, and there's no need to tell Cary, your aunts or anyone else over here about this; it'll just get 'em all worked up; let's keep it between you and me."

"But, Daddy, I think…."

Ray interrupted her and ordered, "Just let sleepin' dogs lie, go on about your business, and let me take care of mine. I assure you, we're all fine over here, so don't stir things up. Please honey, I'm more than a little embarrassed about this and just want you to drop it, OK?"

"I'm sorry, Daddy. I didn't mean to sass you, or be buttin' into your business. I'm just totally confused by all this but if you say drop it, then, of course, I will."

"Thanks sweetheart, I knew you'd do like I told you, once I explained how important it was to me."

CHAPTER 39

Cary Meets a Jazz Man

During the FBI house cleaning at the paper mill, a few of the Klansmen and white supremacists that made threats or attempts to harm Ray and his family had been attested for their actions. While most of these charges were dismissed, the FBI undercover agents made sure that word of the arrests got out on the white supremacist grapevine, and after a few months the Klan leaders declared, "Hey, there ain't no percentage in hasslin' the Simmons's, they're well protected and there's easier targets than them around here."

The crisis that Cary had never known existed had pretty much run its course; he was once again able to answer the phone, roam the woods, hang around the school after classes, and take a more active role in many extracurricular activities.

The FBI agent who had worked as bandmaster at the high school was reassigned, and the current bandmaster, actually a 'band mistress', was a wonderful, compassionate woman and an excellent teacher. With her encouragement, Cary had become drum-major/assistant conductor of the school band. Furthermore, he had formed a jazz band of his own and was beginning to get some paying gigs.

Because he was such a responsible young man, he was given a key to the school band hall; additionally, he was granted permission to hold his jazz band rehearsals there, on evenings when no school activity was scheduled.

Now that Cary was no longer forced to stay so close to home, he began to go target shooting with one of his school chums. When this chum mentioned that he wanted to sell his target pistol, quite cheaply, Cary decided that he just had to have it.

Cary had a very compassionate nature, shared his father's distaste for hunting, never even considered shooting a living thing but, unlike his father, he didn't have a distaste of guns and enjoyed target shooting. Ray's general abhorrence for firearms was so strong that he had never owned a gun or permitted one in his home.

Cary's first attempt to discuss owning a pistol met with immediate rejection by his Daddy; Ray simply refused to hear of permitting Cary to own any type of firearm.

Cary usually accepted his father's decisions with little or no argument; this time however, he didn't. He whined, wheedled and persisted in pleading his case until his father, realizing that this was an important issue for his son, gave in. Therefore, after extracting Cary's solemn vow that he would use the pistol only for target practice or 'plinkin' at inanimate objects, and that he would clean, store and handle the pistol in a responsible and safe manner, Ray allowed Cary to buy the pistol.

Not too long after purchasing the pistol, Cary's school band performed at a Fourth of July celebration on the beach in Fairview; following the band's performance, Cary heard the distant sound of jazz music and went in search of the source. He discovered a trailer equipped with pop-up walls, an upright piano, and a record player hooked up to a speaker system; performing in this trailer was a man named Monty McGee. Monty would play the piano for a while; then, he would spin 78s from his large and impressive collection of Dixieland Jazz records.

A number of years back, Monty McGee had been Turk Murphy's piano player at Punch & Judy's in New Orleans. When Turk became famous, and moved to San Francisco, where he became THE attraction at Earthquake McGoon's, he asked Monty to move out there with him. However, Monty would not even consider moving to the west coast. That was just too far from the "city that time forgot" and the life style that Monty enjoyed, so he remained in New Orleans.

When he reached his late 60s, Monty realized that the rigors of playing Dixieland piano, on a full time basis, were more than he chose to endure, so he retired and moved to Le Grande. He still loved playing piano and entertaining, so when a local bakery offered him a part time job, he accepted. His new job entailed going to public events and promoting the bakery's products; this is what he was doing in Fairview when Cary happened upon him.

Monty became aware of this young boy, in a high school band uniform, who seemed intrigued by his performance; he found it unusual that the boy took such an interest in the type of music he was playing. Most of the kids his age were simply nuts over this horrible new rock-n-roll stuff and looked on jazz with disdain. Curious, Monty called the boy over; while they were talking, one record completed and another one began playing. Monty noticed the boy's attention drift from the conversation to the music, so he inquired, "Do you like that music?"

Cary replied, "Yeah. That's Irving Fazola - probably the greatest clarinet player that ever lived."

Monty was completely taken back by this; only the very hippest aficionados knew about Fazola, who had died in 1949 at the age of 36; he was a gifted musician, but a very temperamental man, who made very few recordings and seldom strayed far from New Orleans. As these two continued talking, Monty learned that Cary knew a great deal about jazz and was dying to learn more.

Monty and Cary quickly became fast friends. Early in the friendship, Cary introduced Monty and his wife, Ethel, to his parents. Ray, as much a Jazz fan as Cary, was delighted to meet and talk music with Monty; Grace liked both of the McGee's immensely. Ray and Grace were delighted that their son had acquired such a fine teacher and friend.

On many occasions Monty and Ethel would take Cary with them on their weekend visits to New Orleans for jam sessions; Monty got a real kick out of Cary's awe at attending these jam sessions and being introduced all around.

Cary met such notables as Pete Fountain, Al Hirt, Mugsy Spanier, Wingy Malone, and others. These talented Jazzmen were thoroughly captivated by this young and eager fan. Often, when one of them would spot him, listening intently and quite obviously mesmerized by their arrangement of a classic Dixieland tune, they would gift him with their original copy of the arrangement. These arrangements were something he could never have purchased at a music store and he treasured them.

CHAPTER 40

Cary Struts His Stuff

High school bands in south Alabama considered it a great honor to be invited to march in the Mardi Gras parades. Competition for the Mardi Gras' Best High School Band award and accompanying trophy was fierce; every band in the parade coveted this award.

The Center High School Band had taken this award, for as long as Cary could remember. Center, a former all black school, was now integrated; however, there were no white kids in its marching band. It was generally accepted, in the south, that the black kids had more rhythm and put on a better show than the white ones did. Most folks just assumed that as long as Center High's band remained all black, it would continue to take the Best Band award.

Cary however subscribed to no such notion; he was determined to lead his school band in knocking the socks off the judges and the crowds during Mardi Gras, and bring the coveted Best Band award home to Fairview High School. To this end, he put in long hours planning his band's program for the Mardi Gras parades.

Using bits and pieces from the original arrangement that he had acquired from the Jazz greats in New Orleans, Cary created his own unique jazzy arrangements of such classics as Tiger Rag, Muskrat Ramble, When the Saints Go Marching In, Millenberg Joys, and others. Next, he choreographed intricate marching routines and he drilled his band, endlessly, until they were able to do these routines almost in their sleep.

During Mardi Gras, this year, each time the Fairview High School Band marched, the crowds lining the streets along the parade route greeted them with cheers and wild applause. Cary and his fellow band members were thrilled by this reaction, and were having the time of their young lives hamming it up for the crowds.

By Fat Tuesday, the final day of Mardi Gras, the parade watchers were captivated by the Fairview High School Band and by Cary. Cary stood six-feet tall (his drum major's hat added over a foot to that); he was reed thin, double jointed, and had been blessed with a natural grace and sense of rhythm.

Cary, feeding on the crowd's energy and approval, was primed and ready. When his band got within sight of the reviewing stand, he halted them momentarily; instructed "OK y'all lets hit that New Orleans lick real hard"; then, prancing, high stepping and strutting like he had never done before in his life, he lead and inspired his band to give a spectacular performance.

The crowd went utterly wild, applauding, cheering, whistling, and stomping feet in time to the music. When Cary saw the judges come to their feet in a standing ovation, he knew that his band had won the competition and to add frosting to the cake,

Cary heard a red neck in the crowd say, "Look at that there white boy go. He puts that nigger drum major from Center High to shame. I'm here to tell y'all that white boy is some kinda' good at struttin'."

Following a band performance at an evening football game, Cary was hitch hiking home when a young black kid pulled his car over to the curb and yelled, "Hey, buddy I see you're wearing a Fairview High band uniform; I play in the band over at the school near Point Clear. Get in and I'll give you a ride. Maybe we can talk a little music along the way."

Cary tossed his clarinet case in the back seat and jumped in; the black kid introduced himself as Monk James.

"Nice wheels, man." Cary exclaimed. "I wish I had my own set."

"My dad's the manager of a bank, over in Le Grande. He got a really good deal on this neat jalopy 'cause the bank repo'ed it and felt it was too old and beat up to resell; so, they offered it to my dad real cheap."

Monk, really enjoying the company of a fellow musician near his age, chattered on, "He said he got it for me 'cause black kids who hitch hike around here are 'puttin themselves in harms way', what ever that means. Usually he's a pretty cool cat but once in awhile he weirds out and says stuff like that."

"Yeah, man I can dig it. My folks are pretty neat, but they sometimes loose their cool like that, too. Guess we just have to go with the flow when the older generation gets weird on us, huh?"

"Not much else you can do, as I see it." responded Monk.

"Man, sometimes my folks get all uptight and don't understand why I haven't outgrown my desire to 'waste good money' on fake vomit or a fake ice cube with a fly in it and other stuff that I get at Bonner Novelty Shop." Cary added, with a grin.

"Holy Cow, do you go there," laughed Monk, "That's the coolest place around. I've got tons of neat stuff from there. You ever try their Sphinx Perfume?"

"Yeah, the foul stuff that smells like raw sewage. Man, you're gonna love this story." Cary chuckled as he began his tale. "You know how crowded the beach around the wharf in Fairview can get on the Fourth of July; well, the dance place and snack bar out on the wharf gets even more crowded. Once when I was a small kid, I wanted a cream soda and a hot dog, and I wanted it NOW but the line was long. Well, I took care of that little problem in a hurry. Do you remember the big fan in one of the snack bar windows? The one covered with a rusty screen to help keep flies out of the motor. Well, I broke out my bottle of Sphinx Perfume, laced that rusty screen with it and within minutes the place was cleared of customers. I marched in and bought my cream soda and hot dog from a clerk who kept saying, "What the hell is that awful smell?"

"Cool man, you were hep even as a little kid and I can't believe you likin' cream soda. Man, I would've lived on that when I was little, if my Mom would've let me."

"Guess we're more alike than we are different, huh?"

"Yeah, I reckon."

"Hey man, what instrument do you play?"

"In the school band, I play drums but that's only because there's no place in the band for an upright bass; that's my real love. I've got a really neat one at home and, if I do say so myself, I'm pretty darn good on it."

"Wow, I'd love to hear you play; I really dig that instrument." Cary volunteered, "I've put together a small jazz band and I'm using a tuba player to cover bass 'cause there aren't many upright bass players around."

"Hey man, it'd be real cool to play in a jazz band. Y'all getting' any gigs, yet?"

Talking music with someone his own age and whose interest where so like his own caused Cary to laughed out loud with sheer joy. "You must really be on my wave length, man; in fact I was just gonna tell you that we're startin' to pick up a few paying gigs, and I live in fear of havin' to cancel one at the last minute because of my tuba player. He's a pretty good cat but really moody; he whines a lot and misses rehearsals when he's - quote - 'not in the mood to play' - unquote; so, I'm, always worried that he'll be a no show at a payin' gig."

"I'd love to sit in with y'all sometimes, unless the rest of your band wouldn't be comfortable havin' a black dude around." Monk offered.

"My guys are a bunch of liberal cats and they wouldn't care if you're green and purple as long as you dig jazz and can play pretty good. We're rehearing on Thursday evening, wanna' sit in then?"

Monk eagerly agreed and, before he dropped Cary off, he got the information about when and where they rehearsed.

Monk and Cary were just a couple of naïve high school teens who had been shielded, by their parents, from much of the turmoil and hatred being created as efforts to integrate the south continued and became more heated. They saw themselves simply as two musicians who wanted to jam a little together; and beyond making sure that members of Cary's band didn't mind having a 'black dude' around, neither of them gave the difference in skin color much thought. The idea that an innocent 'jam session' could cause major repercussions never entered either of their minds.

On Thursday, the tuba player didn't show up, but Monk did, and man did that little group cook. Monk was a natural and all the guys in the jazz band got off on his skill and musicianship. They created great music that night and Cary went home feeling really good about the session and the future of his jazz band. The good vibes lasted all night and Cary went to school the next day feeling elated.

At school, Cary's schoolmates seemed to avoid him like the plague, no one would stop and talk with him in the halls and many of them wouldn't even return his greeting. That afternoon Cary saw a couple of guys from his jazz band in the hall and they stopped to ask if he knew "What's up?"; they had been getting the silent treatment all day too and, like Cary, they had no clue about why.

As Cary was stowing his books in the locker, he overheard one boy say to another, "That Simmons kid sure screwed up; he had a damn nigger in our band hall last night. Hell, he's usually pretty hep, and he's gotta' know better than to do that; you reckon he just don't care?"

It hit Cary like a ton of bricks - the race thing again.

His classmates and teachers acted like the few blacks who attended Fairview High were forced down their throats and they had to put up with them; but, apparently, it was an entirely different thing for a white member of the band to bring a black from another school into their band hall - that, it seemed, they wouldn't tolerate.

CHAPTER 41

The Klan Gets Riled

T he evening after Monk had jammed with Cary's jazz band, Cary still didn't have his feelings sorted out; he felt hurt, confused and unsure of himself; he wanted to talk to his parents but he was so bummed out that he was even questioning their willingness and ability to understand the situation.

During supper, Ray and Grace sensed that something was wrong with their son, and they questioned him about why he was acting droopy; rather than even try to discuss the situation with them, he just said that maybe he was catching a flu bug or something. He just wanted the whole thing to go away so that he didn't have to think about it anymore.

As they were sitting around the table having an after supper cup of coffee, the evening darkness took on an eerie orange glow. Ray looked out the window, took a step back and muttered "Son of a Bitch." Grace and Cary both stood up to see what caused Ray to utter such an unaccustomed oath; what they saw was something none of them was likely to forget.

There was a group of hooded, robed Klansmen standing around a huge burning cross in the middle of their large lawn. Ray's face registered utter disgust; while Grace and Cary looked scared to death. Grace's mouth fell open and she gasped, "Oh my heavens. What's goin' on out there?"

"Shh! Be very quiet and move away form the window." Ray demanded softly; after a few seconds, he quietly asked Cary, "Where's your pistol?"

Cary was as shocked as he had ever been in his life, not just by the morons on his lawn; but more so, by his father's request for the gun.   After a few seconds, he found his voice and whispered, "In my tent."

"Go, silently, out the back way and get it for me.   Be very careful that those nuts out there don't see you."

"OK, I'll be right back." A pale and frightened Cary quickly ran to fetch the pistol.

When Ray had the gun in his hand, he instructed Grace and Cary, "Stay inside and once I'm well around the corner of the trailer, turn off all the inside lights."

Grace and Cary looked at each other aghast and instinctively held hands. They complied with Ray's instructions and stood trembling and clasping hands as they waited to see what would happen next.   They were sure that Ray would not harm the Klansmen, if he could get out of it, but they surmised that under the circumstances he might have to use the gun to defend himself or to protect them.

What happened next was sheer genius on Ray's part.   He slipped up behind a sweet gum tree at the edge of the lawn, the one on which he had mounted a light, way back when they were clearing the land.   He flipped the switch for the light and immediately emptied the pistol, all nine rounds, into the air hitting the light bulb with every shot.

Blinded by the sudden bright light, and startled out of what little wits they possessed, by the sound of Ray firing the pistol; the Klansmen immediately scattered in every direction.   The Simmons's could hear them stumbling around, cussing as the briars, brambles and underbrush ripped their prized robes to ribbons, and as they rushed deeper into the surrounding woods, sounds of them falling and smacking headlong in to trees filled the night air.

If any Klansman among the group had thought to bring a flashlight, they didn't have presence of mind enough to use it or perhaps, because of the unexpected gunfire, they were afraid of becoming easy targets if they used a light.

When the yells and cusses finally subsided into the distance, Ray poured water on the smoldering cross, put on the perimeter lights to discourage any soul brave enough to consider another sneak attack and went back inside.

As he entered the house, he was muttering under his breath, "Damn, I thought all this business was pretty much behind us."

Not realizing that Ray was referring to his action at the mill, Cary ventured, "I think they did this because I had a black kid at my jazz band rehearsal last night."

He reluctantly told his parents of his blunder in inviting Monk into the high school band hall and the reaction that he had experienced at school all day.

Ray reacted to this information in his usual calm manner and commiserated with Cary over his well meant but naïve action. "Son," he said gently, "you pretty much know what you have to do to minimize the impact of this, don't you."

"I reckon I have to tell Monk that we can't play music together any more." Cary said in a trembling voice.

"Unfortunately, that is exactly right. I hate that it comes down to this, but with the political climate and mob mentality that surround race issues down here right now, folks would never allow us, or your friend Monk and his kin, a moment's peace if you try to continue this friendship openly."

Ray walked over to Cary and placed a hand gently on his shoulder, "Son, I wish it didn't have to be like this; I would love for you two young musicians to be able to grow together, but it's just too dangerous for all concerned. I know Monk's family will understand and agree with me. They don't want their son harmed any more than I do."

Dejectedly, Cary phoned Monk early the next morning, explained what had occurred the night before, and gave him the sad news that their promising and eagerly anticipated musical adventure and budding friendship was simply not to be.

Monk, while every bit as sad as Cary about the situation, knew that Cary spoke the truth and that his parents would echo the same thing when they learned what the Simmons's had endured the night before.

The two talented young musicians parted ways and would never know what wonderful music they may have created together if they had met in another time and place.

On Monday, Cary was very contrite and deferential to his teachers and schoolmates. In band class, that afternoon, he apologized for his lapse in judgment. His band mistress accepted the apology with warmth and compassion and did everything she could to reassure Cary that she truly understood and empathized with him. As a female trumpet player of exceptional talent, she had experienced first hand what discrimination could do to the soul; less talented male musicians and orchestra leaders had made her life a living hell until she accepted the fact that circumstances relegated her to rise no higher than high school band instructor.

Federal law enforcement took charge of catching the Klansmen who had terrorized the Simmons family; this was a good thing because a couple of the men involved in this dastardly action were local deputy sheriffs. The FBI had little problem locating and arresting the men involved; most of them were covered with scratches, bruises and cuts; sheeting material from their robes was found in the woods, near the Simmons place, and easily traced back to them.

Once a couple of the men were caught, they began talking and implicating others. One fellow told the arresting officers, "Hell, we never thought Ray could shoot, none of us had ever known of him to do so. We kinda' thought that somebody had tipped off the FBI and we know you bastards are dangerous, that's why we high tailed it out of there so quick."

This incident made a lasting impression on Cary; his last few months in high school were uncomfortable, his pure enjoyment of music was tarnished, and he resolved to finish his senior year, get his diploma, and then, diploma in his hand, he would get the hell out of DIXIE.

Shortly before graduation, Cary took a bus over to Le Grande where he talked with a Navy recruiter about joining up. He was at a bus stop, waiting for the bus to take him back to Parkville, when a young black man, driving a new convertible, drove passed. Cary, deep in thought, took little notice of the car or the driver; but the driver noticed Cary and pulled over to the curb. "Cary Simmons, you ole son-of-a-gun, is that really you?"

Cary looked up and was astonished and delighted to see his childhood buddy Lonnie Morton jumping out of the convertible.

"Lonnie! You're a sight for sore eyes! I don't believe it. How long has it been?" Cary shouted as he pumped Lonnie's hand and slapped him on the back.

"How's your family?" Lonnie wanted to know.

"Doin' OK; of course, Daddy's still at the mill and, from time to time, he fills Grace and me in on what's happenin' with y'all. In fact you're finishin' up school this year, too, aren't you?"

"Finally, man I'm gonna be glad to go to work and make some bread."

"Speakin' of bread, it looks like ole Frank Mason's doin' good. I see he is playin' for the Braves now.

"Yeah, ain't it neat."

Hell, yes, I love it when a local Tannerville kid makes good; your daddy and y'all must be real pleased, too. Remember how your daddy used to hold Frank up to us and say "watch that boy, he's gonna go far. I reckon it's nice to be proved right."

"Hey man, we really are proud of Frank and Tony, too. Tony has got a pretty good start on a baseball career.   When he graduates in May, he's gonna' go down to Tampa and play for a farm team down there."

"That's great, man. In a few years, I'm gonna' be able to tell people 'I knew Frank and Tony Mason, back in Tannerville, when they were just learnin' to play sand lot ball." Cary was enjoying this interlude after all the problems he had been dealing with lately.

"Yeah, man, I might try playin' ball too; who knows, you may even ask for my autograph one day." Lonnie playfully punched Cary on the arm. "What's jivin' with you?"

Cary filled him in on what was going on, including his brief friendship with Monk, the cross burning incident and his resolve to get out of the south.

Lonnie shook his head. "It's some kinda crazy place down here, ain't it? It don't make no sense; I mean, a bunch of crazies burn a cross on the lawn of a white boy who lets a nigger play in his band hall, and then these same crazies turn around and cheer their fool heads off when a nigger hits a home run in a ballgame."

After a little more banter and back slappin; the two childhood friends went their separate ways and each of them was a little happier because of the encounter.

Early in his senior year, Cary had been accepted at Georgia Tech. Ray and Grace were thrilled by this. Cary had friends who were already attending that college and, until his encounter with the Klan, he had looked forward to helping engineer a 'ramblin wreck from Georgia Tech' and other college activities that his friends described to him. After the Klan encounter, no amount of reasoning, pleading or prediction of dire consequences by Ray, Grace, or any of Cary's teachers could induce him to remain in the south and he withdrew his application from that school.

Cary suffered one last disappointment before he was able to make good on his resolve to leave the south. He was looking forward to his graduation ceremony and spending a few weeks relaxing around home before joining the Navy and embarking on this new life; but, again, fate intervened.

A few days before graduation, the FBI learned that the Klan planned to have Cary targeted by a sniper as he marched in his graduation processional; they met with the Simmons family to assure them that they could and would protect Cary, if he opted to participate in the ceremony. However, school officials made it clear that they would rather mail Cary his diploma so that they would not have to expose his classmates and their families to any FBI security procedures.

When Cary learned of this, he gave up on Fairview High, his classmates and all the rest of Dixie. He immediately went to the Navy recruiting office; enlisted, and, on the evening his classmates were getting their diplomas, Cary was on a bus headed for a Navy boot camp in California.

CHAPTER 42

Ray and Grace Alone

After Cary joined the Navy, Ray and Grace completed the land clearing; Ray designed and constructed a beautiful home; Grace created lush flower gardens that soon became the showplace of the neighborhood.

They sorely missed their son; Cary made brief visits home when he could get enough leave time to do so. These visits were bitter-sweet for Ray and Grace; they enjoyed Cary's visits and were pleased and amazed at how quickly he was maturing; nonetheless, they would have preferred to have a happy-go-lucky college boy who spent his summers and school holidays living in Parkville with them.

The last few years had taken their toll on Grace and Ray; they had seen, up close and personal, how greed, envy, bigotry, racial prejudice, and intolerance could bring out the very worst in many folks. They paid dearly for this knowledge, their son had been robbed of much of his youth; many of their neighbors and folks with whom they did business treated them coldly; and they had lost some of their naïve trust in mankind.

During the time Ray worked at the Tannerville mill, he had received many job offers from other mills within the company, as well as, from other companies; many of these jobs were located outside of Alabama and away from the Gulf Coast. Since he and Grace enjoyed life along the Gulf Coast, he never seriously considered any of these offers.

Lately, he had begun to wonder if they would be happier living somewhere other than Parkville; maybe, a change of scenery was what they needed right now.

When an opening occurred at the Pinedale, Arkansas mill and he was offered the job, he didn't immediately dismiss it; instead, he asked for and was granted a couple of weeks to think it over and discuss it with Grace.

"Shorty, a few days ago, I had an interesting offer." Ray began one evening as they sat on the front porch drinking coffee; "Ed's asked me to come up to Pinedale and help him reorganize and modernize the mill up there."

"I don't know Archie; that would mean you'd be gone a lot and I'd be pretty much alone here."

"Guess I didn't make myself clear. The Pinedale mill has become unprofitable and the company has moved Ed up there to be General Manager. They told him to turn things around or they will close that mill. He's gotta' make some massive changes if the mill is to survive and he wants me to transfer up there and help him. This will be a permanent move, he even offered to promote me to PS&D Superintendent, help us find a place to live, and pay movin' expenses."

"Wow, sounds like he's got his work cut out for him; I sure hope he can pull it off."

"You know, Shorty, he was real good to me while he was at the Tannerville mill - went out of his way to give my career a boost; now, he says he really needs me up there and I hate to tell him no."

"Well, that's somethin' to think about, isn't it?" Grace's eyes gleamed with a spark of interest and her full attention was now on Ray.

"Yes, it is. You know until recently I never thought I would want to leave here, but now I'm not sure."

"Some days I feel exactly the same way."

"Yesterday, Ed called again and sweetened the pot a little. He promised that if I'll come up and see the modernization project through, and I don't want to stay in Pinedale after the project is completed, he'll see to it that I get transferred to the mill of my choice at no loss of position or pay. In other words, if we want to come back down here in a couple of years, there'll be no problem."

As Ray talked, he was warming to the idea of taking this job; perhaps he and Grace could find renewed pleasure in life if they lived somewhere else. Grace's response proved that she was thinking along the same lines.

"Archie, I think you should seriously consider this offer. These last few years have been rough and things still aren't right around here."

"Some of the joy has sure been drained out of this place, hasn't it?" Ray agreed.

Grace sighed, "You can say that again; I hate it that we still get angry looks from folks in this town. These, so-called, 'pillars of the community' have no idea what you've contributed to the mill and this community and they sure as hell, don't have any idea of what it cost this family, emotionally, for you to do it. Oh no, folks just remember that you got the local Klan worked up awhile back and, somehow, they figure that makes the whole neighborhood look bad. Hell, you're a real unsung hero and these folks are just too dumb to know it."

"Now Shorty, don't go blowin' things all out of proportion."

"Oh stop being so humble, Archie. You put your job on the line and disrupted all our lives because you knew somebody had to stand up against what was being done to those niggers and you saw that nobody else at that mill was gonna do it. You down played the whole thing; you didn't let me to talk to my family what was goin' on. Even now, you won't let anybody, me included, give you credit for your heroic deeds. Archie, can't you see that I'm proud of you and it's natural that I want to share that pride with the family."

"Shorty, you are makin way too much of the whole thing. I took no pride in helping clean up a mess that never should have existed in the first place, and my motives for keepin' quiet about it aren't as pure as you seem to think. Sure, I wanted to protect you and the kids, but, to put it to you plainly, I just didn't want to face how some of our kin would react. You know that lots of 'em wouldn't have liked what I was doin'."

"I doubt that there would have been as many against it as you think."

"Well, I still don't want to know about how many would have lined up against me or how far they would have gone in their efforts to stop me. I think it best to just let sleepin' dogs lie and not push your kin unless you absolutely have to. In my mind, that makes me more coward than hero."

"You're wrong, Archie, but I'll shut up about it. Maybe a new place is what we need. It would be nice to go fishin' somewhere that didn't have so many memories of good times shared with Cary. I swear, sometimes when I catch a big fish, I look around expectin' him to be there sayin', 'Good catch, it's a keeper'. When I realize I'm alone; it takes some of the thrill out of it for me. I wonder how the fishin' is in Pinedale."

"Let's take Ed up on his job offer; it'll be fun to find out about the fishin and to see what else Pinedale can offer us, don't you think? We might even learn to like it bein' just the two of us with no kids around." Ray had a twinkle in his eye and sounded more animated and excited than he had been in quite awhile.

"Yeah, let's do it!" Grace called over her shoulder; she was humming as she left the room to begin rounding up luggage and packing material.

With a sense of adventure and renewed hope, Ray and Grace went off to Arkansas to start another chapter in their lives.

CHAPTER 43

Comin' Home

After the modernization project at the Pinedale mill was completed, Ray's job became less challenging and he became restless. Somehow, his work, his life and even the fishin' in Arkansas was not as fulfilling or as enjoyable as he had hoped.

Except for the year that Ray spent traveling the western United States when he was in his late teens, and the business trips he had taken later in his life, he had never been away from the Gulf Coast.

Ray often thought of the Gulf Coast; he remembered his and Grace's kin, a multitude of good friends and the good times he and Grace had shared raising their kids down there. Eventually, he recognized that he was homesick and began pondering what he should do about it.

One afternoon, instead of following his usual routine of grabbing a beer and sitting in front of the TV to watch the 5 o'clock news, he wandered into the kitchen where Grace was preparing their dinner. Grace was surprised to see him there, and even more surprised when he told her what was on his mind. "Shorty, how would you feel about heading back home?"

She gave him a puzzled look. "You mean go to Alabama and visit your Momma and the rest of the folks?"

"No, I mean move back down there. I just learned that the PS&D Superintendent at the mill in Dawns Ferry Mississippi is retiring and I'm thinking that I might like that job, if it's alright with you."

"Actually, it's more than alright, I'd love it. I've enjoyed bein' up here but it's not really home, is it?"

"Nope, it's not. I miss bein' able to just drop in on family; I miss surf fishin; I miss smellin' the salty Gulf air; hell, I even miss smellin' swampy old Choctaw Creek."

"So, are you gonna' talk to Ed about transferring?"

"Now that I know you're OK with it; you bet I am."

Ray took the job in Dawns Ferry; he and Grace bought a home on the banks of the Singing River. It had a huge back yard so that they could garden - Grace concentrating on flowers and Ray raising vegetables. The little town of Dawns Ferry suited them just fine; they made some wonderful friends and settled into an easy, enjoyable life style. They bought a boat; large enough so that they could sleep on board and stay out on the water for a couple of days, but was small enough so that they could crew it without help.

The second year they lived in Dawns Ferry, they threw a Gumbo and Lobster Feed for Ray's staff at the mill, a few neighbors, and members of the local Fire Department. Everyone raved about this party; so, Ray and Grace decided to make it an annual affair. Grace, usually shy and uncomfortable in a crowd, unexplainably gloried as hostess of this event and took great pride in preparing it.

Folks who attended the Gumbo Feed, bragged about what a great party it was; the firemen asked if they could bring their wives, Ray's bosses at the mill hinted broadly that they would like to be included and, of course, Ray said OK, and so it went.

The Gumbo Feed just kept growing over the years and preparing for it became a huge task. One year, Ray decided that Grace needed help putting on a party this size; without consulting her, he took it upon himself to get her some help. One day, seemingly out of the blue, he brought his secretary over to the house and announced to Grace that she was going to assist with the party plans. Grace wasn't happy about this, but she saw no way to say so without embarrassing Ray.

Grace and the secretary had very different ideas about what made a successful party; Grace instinctively knew that she should do things her way. However, to avoid appearing to be a overbearing boss's wife, she gave in on many issues.

"Ok, Debbie Sue, here's the game plan; we'll cover Ray's potting table with a pretty plastic table cloth, set out some snacks on it; line a couple of wheelbarrows with aluminum foil, put ice in 'em and put one at each end of the snack table; one we'll fill with soft drinks and the other with beer. This way everybody can just wander over, grab a drink and a snack, mingle with each other or check out Ray's vegetable garden until he and Jack get the lobster ready to serve.

"Oh no ma'am, the women don't need to be out in the yard with all this heat, listenin' to all the work talk and corny mill jokes them ole boys will be tellin'. You have such a pretty livin' room and the house is all air conditioned and everything. Let's set up a punch bowl and a tray of little finger sandwiches in the dinin' room and I can serve them while we have 'girl talk' till the meal is ready."

"I'm not so sure about doin' it that way, everybody seems to like to be together and it's really not that hot this early in the spring."

"Trust me Miz Simmons, I give parties all the time and this is the best way."

"Well OK, if you really think that's the best way, that's how we'll do it."

The party that year was not up to its usual standard, the mood was not as relaxed and festive as usual, and many of the guests left early. Grace was embarrassed and frustrated by the party's lack of success, and as soon as the last guest had departed, she took her frustrations out on Ray.

"I hope you're satisfied."

Ray failed to notice the sarcasm in Grace's voice and didn't yet know that he was in the dog house "No Shorty, I'm not. This party just wasn't right somehow; I can't put my finger on what went wrong; but, I know that it wasn't up to par."

"I'll tell you what was wrong. Your secretary is what was wrong. Her insistin' "everybody will like it better if the women stay in the livin' room sharin' finger sandwiches and 'girl talk' while the 'boys' hang out by the Gumbo pot. That's what's wrong."

"Well don't take my head off, you shouldda' just told her how you wanted it done and made her do it that way."

"Oh yeah, I shouldda' just played Miz Bitchy Bosses Wife and ordered her around. Archie, you told her to assist me; so she figured she had some say in how to run the thing."

"Don't make me the heavy in all this." Ray laughed; but Grace was in no mood to laugh with him or let him off the hook.

She ranted and railed at him awhile longer and made her position very clear. "If you ever again get anyone to assist me with another Gumbo Feed, I'll cancel the whole damn thing. I mean it Ray; that's my final word on the subject."

Grace seldom disagreed with Ray's decisions, much less railed at him and, a blind man could see that this year's party had not been a rousing success. "I'm didn't mean to screw up your party, Shorty. I see now that askin' Debbie Sue to help was not very smart. I'm really sorry. I know how you love plannin' and hostessin' this shindig, and everybody says you're real good at it; so, I promise not to help you again unless you tell me to."

The next year Grace did the Gumbo Feed her way and redeemed herself as hostess; the party was outstanding and the guests toasted her often and lavishly.

CHAPTER 44

Ray Won't Talk

When he reached his late fifties, it became important to Ray that he preserve the family history, as he remembered it; always a wonderful storyteller, he chose to do this by sharing family stories and memories with his kids, grandkids, nieces, nephews and old family friends each time they visited him.

Many of Ray's stories illustrated how he loved and held his father in high regard; he inevitably portrayed his father as a good, loving, and dependable man; never once did he make any mention of his father's racist beliefs or involvement in the Klan.

In his oral family history lessons, Ray never included anything about the turmoil at the paper mill, in the 1950's & 1960's, or his role in gaining fair treatment for the black workers there. Ray's unwillingness to talk about this frustrated Jo. She felt very strongly that this part of the family history should be preserved; she longed to know and understand the extent of her Daddy's role in redressing the civil wrongs committed against the blacks at the mill.

From the time of the incident in Georgia, Jo closely followed the civil rights activity; she listened to TV accounts, and read everything that appeared in the newspaper, magazine articles and books on the subject. Of course, there were misunderstandings, inaccuracies and false portrayals in much of the recorded material. She had witnessed enough of civil rights events to know that what was reported didn't reflect these events accurately and some of the things published were downright untruths; still, she wondered why she could find absolutely no mention of her Daddy in anything she read.

Once, in the late nineteen sixties, she asked her Daddy why there was no record of his involvement; his curt reply shocked her. "Because I only did what had to be done, I purposely tried to keep myself out of the papers and off TV, and I don't want anyone - you included to glamorize or call attention to it now."

Somehow, despite her Daddy's rebuff, Jo wasn't content to let the matter drop and over the years, she would occasionally try to appeal to his desire to preserve family history as a ploy to get him to talk about it.

"Daddy, please talk to me about what happened at the paper mill to bring in the FBI and get the Klan so riled up. My kids have a right to know how their Grandpa fought to uphold civil rights, even when these issues were unpopular and defending them was a dangerous thing to do."

"Jo, there's no need for them to know more about that mess than what's already written in the history books"

"But Daddy, there's nothing in those books about what you did and that's what I want my kids to know."

"Honey, they don't need to hear about all that ugliness, it took place in a different world and it needs to remain back in that world. Don't pester me about it anymore because I'm not going to change my mind."

Reluctantly, Jo gave in and honored her Daddy's wishes; she curbed her curiosity and let the matter drop. She concluded that her Daddy's reluctance to talk might have been motivated by his desire to protect his father's privacy. Perhaps, knowing that his grandchildren would have limited understanding of the way of life that existed in the South during their great grandfather lifetime, he felt that they would judge his Klan affiliation too harshly.

Another possibility, that crossed Jo's mind, was that her Daddy feared the action he had taken on behalf of the black mill workers would be interpreted, by some, as his way of showing disrespect for his father and he certainly wanted nobody to come to that erroneous conclusion.

CHAPTER 45

Sibling Reunion

By the mid 1970's Cary had decided that the Navy was not the career he wanted; hence, he became a civilian, settled in Hawaii, and married.

During his Navy years, Cary had seen little of his sister Jo; they sporadically exchanged phone calls and letters, but were rarely able to manage a real visit. Jo was pleased to get a phone call from her brother and pleasantly surprised by what he said. "Hey Sis, I've gotta be in southern California on business; any chance that you could fly down and meet me there?"

Jo's first marriage had failed. She was now married to a third generation California native. She was living in the San Francisco

Bay Area and happily juggling a budding career in telecommunications, raising her children, managing her household, and attending evening classes at a local college.

With no thought about how she would arrange to fly to southern California on such a short notice, Jo told her brother, "Oh hell, YES, I wouldn't let you get this close to me and not grab a chance to visit with you."

On the flight out of Honolulu, Cary's seatmate inquired, "What takes you to southern California?"

"I'm seeking a publisher and visiting with my sister." Cary, a tall slender man in his early thirties, responded.

"What are you trying to get published that requires you to leave the Islands? Surely, there are plenty of adequate publishers here."

"True; but none of them seem to share my goal." The slender young man replied. He then explained how he and his wife spent several years researching and re-constructing an ancient Hawaiian time-keeping system. Taking great care to ensure the accuracy and authenticity of this unique system, they had conducted their research under the close guidance and tutelage of the Kupuna and had the completed project reviewed by researchers at the University of Hawaii. "The goal", explained, "is to present this system to the world in a way that shows the richness and breadth of the Hawaiians' arts & sciences. Local publishing houses seem blind to this goal and want to change it into a tourist-oriented gimmick; hence, I'm searching for a publisher who will respect our desires."

"Good luck. It sounds like something that's well worth preserving. I hope you're successful."

When the plane landed at the Burbank Airport, Cary was among the first to deplane; he spotted his sister and called out, "Over here, Jo".

Jo turned toward the voice, squealed and walked into the welcoming arms of her only brother. After a big bear hug, the two siblings pulled apart and gave each other a good long look. Cary was the first to speak. "Wow, you look great; it seems forever since I've seen you."

"You are a sight for sore eyes yourself. I've missed you like crazy." Jo linked her arm with Cary's, and arm in arm they walked toward the terminal.

"Do you have any checked luggage?"

"Nope, I'm traveling light - just my carry on bag and brief case."

"I've booked rooms at a hotel right here in Burbank; since the TV show, Laugh In, made beautiful downtown Burbank a household word, I thought it would be a kick to stay here even though there appears to be no "downtown Burbank" the area does have a lot of charm. Also, it seems to be mid-way between the publishing houses you're planning to see."

"Cool, Sis; how's your family? I bet the kids are growing like weeds, I want to hear all about them and about that husband of yours?"

"I brought pictures; we'll look at them later, and I'll fill you in on what they're all up to."

"I'm counting on it."

"Oh Lord! I'm happy to be here; between family, my job, and going to school, I don't get much goof off time. I'm over the moon about having a couple of days to relax, enjoy your company, and have some good long talks."

"I know what you mean; so many times I've wanted your advice on something, other times I've just plain missed sharing a story or a laugh with you."

"So much has happened in the last few years. You deciding to leave the Navy, I mean, after eight years, what a surprise; you getting married, just about the time I was beginning to believe that you were a confirmed bachelor; my divorce and re-marriage; and, only The Lord knows how many other things. I can't tell you how many times that I wanted to hop a plane, go to wherever you were, and just talk your ear off."

The first evening that they were in Burbank, Jo and Cary went to a quaint little pub near their hotel. A long ornately carved bar gleamed in the pub's soft lighting and cast a warm reflected glow into the beautifully gilded mirror that hung behind it; a few tables surrounded a small dance floor and half a dozen mahogany high backed booths lined the back wall.

"Oh, wish that Margaret Ann were with us; she would love this place." Jo exclaimed as they entered the pub.

"Yes she sure would, and I too wish she was here; but running a charter boat business is no easy task. When I spoke with her last week, she said that they were swamped with reservations for deep sea fishin' trips. She really wanted to be here with us but she didn't feel that she should leave John to cope with all the office work on top of overseeing the boat crew."

"You ever think it's ironic that she is the one who ended in the fishin' business?" Jo asked.

"Not really, she's been around boats all her life; startin' with Grandma Simmons father and brothers; then, Daddy and Uncle Wilton always managed to own a boat of some sort." Cary pointed out. "But, when we all went fishin' with Grace and Daddy, she didn't seem as excited as you and me."

"Aw Jo, she's just more like Daddy and Aunt Lilly Ann than either of us are; you know, quiet, kinda dignified, and a bit on the reserved side."

"I reckon you're right; Grace used to tease me by sayin' the doctor accidentally vaccinated me with a phonograph needle and I hadn't stopped talkin' since."

"Well, one thing's for sure folks never had to wonder when you got excited; folks for a mile around you could hear you squeal; now Margaret Ann's different; you've got to look at her to tell if she is really enjoyin' herself; when she is, you can see her eyes sparkle and she gets a little grin on her face."

Cary and Jo opted to sit in one of the high backed booths; they ordered a light meal and, when they had finished eating, a lanky young waiter removed their dinner dishes and inquired; "May I get you an after dinner drink?"

Cary responded, "Have you any Chivas Regal, Royal Salute?"

The young waiter raised his eyebrows. "We don't get much call for that; let me check."

As the waiter walked away, Cary explained to his sister. "During my first Navy tour in Europe, a shipmate introduced me to this magnificent scotch. It isn't very popular here in the U.S. but if they have it, I would really like you to try it. I believe you'll like its unique flavor."

"Sounds wonderful." Jo smiled, liking the new mature sophistication that she noticed in her once naïve 'baby' brother.

The waiter reappeared; "You're in luck, we do have it."

"Great. We'll each have some on the rocks."

As they sat sipping their scotch, they caught up on the current events in each of their lives, went through the 'whatever happened to' routine, laughed over the deeds and misdeeds of their youth, and began reminiscing about their parents.

Remembering their rather unorthodox upbringing, Jo chuckled. "We sure weren't a typical southern family, were we?"

"We were different alright. Yet, I never felt that our lives were missing anything; I actually felt our lives were a little more interesting than most."

"Uh-huh, and it was fun having the most modern thinking Mom around. Grace never cared that all the other ladies wore starched house dresses; she was happy in shorts or jeans, and she would much rather go fishin' than sit on the porch drinking iced tea and gossiping." Jo laughed with affection as she remembered her stepmother's ways. "Remember how some of the church members would get all upset over the fact that our folks fished on Sunday, and that some Sunday's they even had the gall to let us kids miss Sunday School to go with them."

Cary grinned, "Yeah, funny thing is I felt as close to God sitting on the beach, watching the sunrise over a beautiful body of water, as I did in Sunday school, didn't you?"

"Yep; I still do."

They both fell silent, each of them absorbed in their memories. Finally, Clay ventured; "I imagine that Daddy was one of less than a handful of white men in south Alabama who, by word and deed, taught his kids to respect blacks."

Jo nodded, "It's a good thing that he did; 'because very few other folks, including preachers and Sunday School teachers, ever seemed sincere when they talked about how Jesus loved all the children, regardless of their color. You know, what I mean; not many of them gave more than lip service to treating black folks with respect."

"Well, Daddy sure walked what he talked; probably more than either of us realized."

"I'm sure you're right about that; I wish that I could get him to tell me about the stuff that he was involved in at the paper mill back in the '50's, but every time I try to get him to talk about it, he gets uncharacteristically stubborn and downright curt in his refusal."

Assuming that their Daddy talked more freely about this with Cary than he would with her, she asked, "What does Daddy say when y'all talk about it?"

"We don't talk about it. Every time I attempt to introduce the subject, all he will say is 'let sleeping dogs lie'. Then he changes the subject so quick that it makes my head spin."

"Cary, you must remember more than I do; you were still livin' at home when all this stuff was goin' on. At least, tell me about when Daddy got the Ku Klux Klan so frustrated that they threatened to kill all of us?"

"Good Lord, I'll never forget that." Cary frowned and shook his head, as if, even after all this time, he still couldn't quite believe what had happened. "You see Jo, it's like this, Daddy and Grace kept me pretty shielded from a lot of what was goin' on at the time, and in my ignorance, I inadvertently played a role in causin' those Klan threats." Cary turned pale, his eyes welled with tears and his hand trembled as he played with his empty glass. "I'm here to tell you, Sis, that incident changed the entire direction of my life."

Jo knew instinctively that Cary needed to unburden himself and she sure wanted to hear what he had to say. "Order us a fresh drink and start talking; I want to know everything."

"Aw hell, I'm sure there is much about that time that I still don't know; like I just said, the folks pretty much shielded me at the time; Daddy still won't talk to me about what was going on at the mill during those years. Over the years, I've visited the Quarters and managed to find some folks still livin' there that worked at the mill with Daddy and were willing talk to me about it; I've used the Freedom of Information Act to conduct some research, so I've pretty much pieced most of what happened."

"Since you never asked about this before now, I figured that you shared Daddy's "let sleepin' Dogs lie" attitude about it; so I just kept what I learned to myself. God, it is gonna to be good to finally share it with you."

So, at long last, Jo learned that her Daddy was truly a hero - a reluctant hero - but a hero nonetheless.

Epilogue

Raymond Archibald Simmons is my beloved Daddy. He physically departed this world in 1995 but his spirit lives on; I hope that his spirit will touch the hearts of many others as it has my own. A man of my Daddy's integrity is so rare; I feel compelled to share his story with the world - even though I know that he would not have approved my doing so.

Sorry to disobey you Daddy but I think you understand.

Nancy Josephine Simmons.

Betty Freeman Haines, a newspaper columnist and curriculum designer, comes from a long line of great storytellers; when her kin are together, they share family stories and folklore as easily as water flows downhill in a creek bed. Betty's passion is creating fictional short stories; she has always known that one day she would write a novel.

Born in Chickasaw, Alabama and raised in a series of small south Alabama mill towns, has etched Betty's brain with memories and insights of attempts to abolish segregation, integrate public schools, and implement equal rights in the work places and voting booths of the Deep South.

For her debut fiction novel, Betty creates a tender tale that presents, to her readers, her small town childhood, the Civil Rights Movement, and the actions of a very special reluctant hero of that era.

Betty and her husband, Vern – who is her best buddy – reside in Mesquite, Nevada. Together they enjoy cooking, gardening, and traveling. Betty, of course, enjoys writing, and, not surprisingly, Vern enjoys proofreading her work.

ISBN: 978-0-615-33436-3

www.ingramcontent.com/pod-product-compliance
Lightning Source LLC
Chambersburg PA
CBHW060239100426
42742CB00011B/1576